TASTE THE
MEDITERRANEAN

Discover the Secrets of Traditional Pizza and Pasta Making.
Easy, Healthy Recipes with Expert Nutritional Guidance.

Alexa Amalfi

TABLE OF CONTENTS

INTRODUCTION

Welcome to the culinary delights of the Mediterranean! Embark on a gastronomic journey through the vibrant flavors and rich traditions of this enchanting region with the Mediterranean Pizza and Pasta Cookbook.

Within the pages of this cookbook, you will discover a treasure trove of delectable recipes that celebrate the art of crafting mouthwatering pizzas and tantalizing pasta dishes inspired by the sun-soaked shores and bountiful harvests of the Mediterranean.

Immerse yourself in the aromas of fresh basil, ripe tomatoes, fragrant olive oil, and zesty spices as you explore the diverse culinary landscapes of Italy, Greece, Spain, and beyond. Each recipe is thoughtfully curated to capture the essence of Mediterranean cuisine, ensuring an authentic and unforgettable dining experience.

Flip through the beautifully illustrated pages and allow your senses to be captivated by images that showcase the vibrant colors and enticing textures of these Mediterranean creations. From classic Margherita pizza adorned with creamy mozzarella and aromatic basil leaves to hearty pasta dishes infused with Mediterranean staples like olives, feta cheese, and sun-drenched vegetables, this cookbook offers a wide array of recipes to suit every taste and occasion.

Whether you're a seasoned chef or a novice home cook, the Mediterranean Pizza and Pasta Cookbook is designed to guide and inspire you. Each recipe is accompanied by easy-to-follow instructions, helpful tips, and variations, making it accessible to cooks of all levels. Learn the secrets to making perfectly crispy pizza crusts, homemade pasta sauces bursting with flavor, and creative topping combinations that will impress your family and friends.

Gather your loved ones around the table, and transport them to the sun-kissed shores of the Mediterranean with your culinary creations. Whether you're hosting a casual dinner party, preparing a quick and nutritious weeknight meal, or simply craving a taste of the Mediterranean, this cookbook will be your trusted companion.

So, open the Mediterranean Pizza and Pasta Cookbook, and let the tantalizing aromas and vibrant flavors elevate your cooking to new heights. With its collection of irresistible recipes, you'll have the power to bring the taste of the Mediterranean into your own kitchen and create memorable meals that will transport you to this captivating region time and time again. Get ready to savor the essence of the Mediterranean and embark on a culinary adventure like no other.

The Art and Science of Mediterranean Pizza Making

Making a Mediterranean pizza is not just about throwing together a few ingredients on a dough base. It's an art form, steeped in tradition and rules that have been perfected over centuries. This chapter will delve into the heart of this art form, exploring the essential rules for crafting authentic Mediterranean pizza.

The first rule is the selection of ingredients. True Mediterranean pizzas rely on fresh, high-quality, and locally-sourced ingredients. Common ingredients include tomatoes, olives, olive oil, mozzarella cheese, and basil, all of which contribute to a rich, distinct flavor profile.

Following the ingredients, the second rule is the dough preparation. A traditional Mediterranean pizza boasts a thin, crisp crust with a slightly chewy texture. Achieving this requires careful handling of the dough, from the right ratio of flour to water and yeast, to the duration for kneading and resting the dough.

The third rule involves the cooking process. Authentic Mediterranean pizza is cooked in a wood-fired oven, producing a unique smoky flavor and a perfectly charred crust. The high heat of the oven also ensures quick cooking, which helps to preserve the freshness and flavor of the ingredients.

Lastly, simplicity is key when it comes to Mediterranean pizza. Each ingredient should shine on its own and not be overwhelmed by too many flavors, embodying the Mediterranean philosophy of 'less is more'. A well-made Mediterranean pizza is a testament to the harmony of quality ingredients, well-thought-out preparation, and meticulous cooking.

By adhering to these rules, you'll be well on your way to mastering the art of Mediterranean pizza making. Each pizza you create will not just be a culinary delight, but also a tribute to the rich, vibrant Mediterranean tradition.

The Principles and Practice of Mediterranean Pasta Making

Creating authentic Mediterranean pasta is a fine balance between precision and creativity. Like the artistry of Mediterranean pizza, pasta making also abides by certain rules, which when followed, result in a genuinely flavorful and satisfying dish.

The first rule in Mediterranean pasta making is choosing the right type of pasta. The Mediterranean region boasts an array of pasta types, each suited for a specific kind of sauce or preparation style. For example, spaghetti is traditionally paired with tomato-based sauces, while penne or fusilli are more suited for chunky and vegetable-based sauces.

The second rule revolves around the sauce. The sauce is the soul of a pasta dish, and Mediterranean cuisine treasures its sauces. Traditional sauces, such as the Marinara, are made with ripe tomatoes, fresh basil, and extra virgin olive oil. A cardinal rule here is never to overpower the pasta with sauce. Instead, the sauce should coat the pasta lightly, enhancing rather than overwhelming its flavor.

The third rule is about the cooking of the pasta itself - "al dente." This Italian term refers to pasta that is cooked to be firm when bitten. Overcooked pasta loses its texture and ends up being mushy, which is a big no in authentic Mediterranean cooking.

Finally, the fourth rule is about the use of fresh, locally-sourced, and seasonal ingredients. Mediterranean pasta dishes often feature fresh vegetables, cheeses, herbs, and seafood, all contributing to a broad and vibrant palate of flavors.

By following these principles, you can master the art of Mediterranean pasta making. Each dish you prepare will be a celebration of simple ingredients, thoughtfully put together, creating a symphony of flavors that is the essence of Mediterranean cuisine.

The Main Rules For The Mediterranean Diet

The first cardinal rule in Mediterranean diet cooking revolves around the use of fresh, local, and seasonal produce. The emphasis is on a variety of fruits, vegetables, whole grains, legumes, and nuts. The freshness of the ingredients used ensures maximum nutritional value, and the broad variety ensures a balanced diet.

The second rule pertains to the choice of fats. Unlike other diets that shun fat, the Mediterranean diet endorses the use of healthy fats, such as olive oil and avocados. Olive oil, in particular, is a staple in Mediterranean cooking, used generously in salads, pasta, and bread.

The third rule is the moderate consumption of dairy and poultry, and limiting red meat. Yogurt, cheese, and poultry are consumed in moderate portions daily to weekly, while red meat is eaten sparingly.

The fourth rule encourages the consumption of fish and seafood, rich in heart-healthy omega-3 fatty acids. In Mediterranean cuisine, fish and seafood are a primary protein source, consumed at least twice a week.

Lastly, the Mediterranean diet promotes the enjoyment of meals with others. Food is often seen as a communal experience, taken in the company of family and friends. This not only enhances the enjoyment of the meal but also encourages mindful eating.

In essence, Mediterranean diet cooking is about celebrating fresh ingredients, savoring flavors, and enjoying the eating experience in good company. It is not just a diet, but a lifestyle — a holistic approach to health and well-being.

The Mediterranean diet is more than just a meal plan, it's a lifestyle. Embracing this diet involves implementing a few key principles:

1. **Prioritize Fruits, Vegetables, and Whole Grains:** The foundation of the Mediterranean diet is plant-based foods. Aim to fill half your plate with fruits and vegetables, and make whole grains the staple of your meals.

2. **Healthy Fats are Your Friends:** Healthy fats, like those found in olive oil, avocados, and nuts, are a hallmark of the Mediterranean diet. Use olive oil as your primary source of added fat, and eat at least two servings of avocado and a small handful of nuts each day.

3. **Fish and Poultry over Red Meat:** Seafood and poultry are the main sources of animal protein. Aim to consume fish twice a week and limit red meat to only a few times a month.

4. **Dairy in Moderation:** Dairy products, particularly cheese and yogurt, are staples in the Mediterranean diet, but are consumed in moderation. Aim for a serving of dairy each day but avoid processed dairy products.

5. **Enjoy Meals with Others:** The social aspect of eating is a key component of the Mediterranean lifestyle. Try to share meals with family and friends as much as possible.

6. **Stay Active:** Regular physical activity is another cornerstone of the Mediterranean lifestyle. Aim for at least 30 minutes of moderate-intensity exercise every day.

By following these principles, you will be well on your way to adopting the Mediterranean lifestyle and reaping its numerous health benefits.

CHAPTER 1:
CLASSIC PIZZA
RECIPES

MARGHERITA PIZZA

- Total Cooking Time: 20-25 minutes
- Prep Time: 10 minutes
- Servings: 4

Ingredients:

- 1 pound (450g) pizza dough
- 1/2 cup pizza sauce
- 2 cups shredded mozzarella cheese
- 2 large tomatoes, sliced
- Fresh basil leaves, torn
- Extra virgin olive oil
- Salt and pepper to taste

Directions:

1. Before you begin, make sure to preheat your oven to a temperature of 475°F (245°C). In case you have a pizza stone, it's recommended to place it inside the oven during the preheating process.

2. After using a rolling pin to achieve an even thickness, carefully transfer the flattened dough onto a baking sheet lined with parchment paper. Alternatively, if you're using a pizza stone, you can transfer it onto a pizza peel before placing it in the oven.

3. Evenly distribute the pizza sauce over the dough, making sure to leave a small border along the edges. Sprinkle half of the mozzarella cheese over the sauce.

4. Arrange the tomato slices neatly on the cheese, creating an organized presentation. Season with salt and pepper to taste. Sprinkle the remaining mozzarella cheese over the tomatoes.

5. Carefully transfer the pizza into the preheated oven. If using a baking sheet, place it directly on the oven rack. When using a pizza stone, transfer the pizza onto the preheated stone by sliding it.

6. Cook for a duration of 12-15 minutes, or until the crust achieves a golden brown color and the cheese is melted and lightly browned.

7. Take the pizza out of the oven and allow it to cool for a brief period. Sprinkle torn basil leaves over the top. Drizzle with extra virgin olive oil.

8. Slice the Margherita pizza into desired portions and serve hot.

Nutritional breakdown per serving:

Calories: 320 kcal, Protein: 14 grams, Carbohydrates: 39 grams, Fat: 12 grams, Saturated Fat: 6 grams, Cholesterol: 30 milligrams, Sodium: 600 milligrams, Fiber: 2 grams, and Sugar: 4 grams.

NEAPOLITAN PIZZA

- Total Cooking Time: 90-120 minutes
- Prep Time: 20 minutes
- Servings: 4

Ingredients:

For the Dough:

- 3 1/2 cups (500g) Tipo 00 flour
- 1 1/2 cups warm water
- 2 teaspoons salt
- 1/2 teaspoon active dry yeast

For the Toppings:

- 1 cup San Marzano tomato sauce
- 2 cups fresh mozzarella cheese, torn into small pieces
- Fresh basil leaves
- Extra virgin olive oil
- Salt to taste

Directions:

1. Blend the flour and salt with the yeast mixture, either using a wooden spoon or your hands, until the ingredients combine and form a sticky dough.
2. Add the flour and salt to the yeast mixture. Mix with a wooden spoon or your hands until a sticky dough forms.
3. Place the dough onto a floured surface and knead it for approximately 10 minutes until it achieves a smooth and elastic texture. Then, shape the dough into a ball.
4. To proceed, carefully return the dough to the bowl and ensure it is covered with a fresh kitchen towel. Allow the dough to rise undisturbed in a warm and draft-free area for an estimated duration of 1 to 2 hours, or until it has visibly doubled in size. This crucial step ensures optimal fermentation and a light, fluffy texture in the final product.
5. To achieve optimal results, preheat your oven to its maximum temperature of around 500°F (260°C). If available, place a pizza stone in the oven during preheating for ideal baking conditions.

6. Once the dough has completed its rising process, divide it into four equal portions. Take each portion and shape it into a round ball, then allow them to rest for approximately 20 minutes.

7. Place one ball of dough on a surface sprinkled with flour. Using your fingertips, delicately stretch the dough into a circular shape, ensuring the edges are slightly thicker than the center.

8. Transfer the stretched dough onto a pizza peel or a parchment-lined baking sheet. If you are using a pizza stone, make sure to sprinkle some flour or cornmeal on the peel to prevent sticking.

9. Spread a thin layer of tomato sauce onto the dough, leaving a small border around the edges. Add the torn mozzarella cheese evenly over the sauce.

10. Take caution as you transfer the pizza onto the preheated pizza stone or baking sheet. Proceed to bake for approximately 8-10 minutes, or until the crust has expanded and turned a beautiful golden brown color.

11. Once the pizza is ready, carefully remove it from the oven and adorn it with freshly-picked basil leaves. Give it a final touch by drizzling some extra virgin olive oil and sprinkling a pinch of salt to elevate the flavors.

12. Repeat steps 7-11 with the remaining dough and toppings to make the remaining pizzas.

Nutritional breakdown per serving:

Calories: 350 kcal, Protein: 15 grams, Carbohydrates: 50 grams, Fat: 9 grams, Saturated Fat: 4 grams, Cholesterol: 20 milligrams, Sodium: 650 milligrams, Fiber:24 grams, and Sugar: 1 grams.

MEDITERRANEAN VEGGIE PIZZA

- Total Cooking Time: 30-35 minutes
- Prep Time: 15 minutes
- Servings: 4

Ingredients:

- 1 pound (450g) pizza dough
- 1/2 cup hummus
- 1 cup baby spinach leaves
- 1/2 cup sliced black olives
- 1/2 cup sliced red bell peppers
- 1/2 cup sliced red onions
- 1/2 cup crumbled feta cheese
- 1 tablespoon chopped fresh oregano
- Extra virgin olive oil
- Salt and pepper to taste

Directions:

1. Before you begin, ensure that your oven is preheated to 475°F (245°C). If you happen to have a pizza stone, you can place it in the oven as it preheats for optimal results.
2. To get the pizza dough ready, sprinkle a generous amount of flour onto a surface and roll it out to your desired thickness. After rolling it out, take care as you transfer the dough onto a baking sheet that has been lined with parchment paper, or onto a pizza peel if you're using a pizza stone.
3. To evenly distribute the hummus, spread it over the dough, making sure to leave a small border around the edges. Layer the baby spinach leaves on top of the hummus.
4. Arrange the sliced black olives, red bell peppers, and red onions over the spinach. Sprinkle the crumbled feta cheese and chopped fresh oregano on top of the vegetables. Season with salt and pepper to taste.
5. Carefully transfer the pizza into the preheated oven. If using a baking sheet, place it directly on the oven rack. If you're using a pizza stone, carefully slide the pizza onto the preheated stone.
6. Baking the pizza for approximately 12 to 15 minutes will result in a crust that is beautifully golden brown and cheese that is fully melted and lightly browned.
7. After taking the pizza out of the oven, allow it to cool for a few minutes before drizzling it with a generous amount of extra virgin olive oil.
8. Slice the Mediterranean veggie pizza into desired portions and serve hot.

Nutritional breakdown per serving:

Calories: 280 kcal, Protein: 10 grams, Carbohydrates: 39 grams, Fat: 10 grams, Saturated Fat: 3.5 grams, Cholesterol: 10 milligrams, Sodium: 650 milligrams, Fiber: 4 grams, and Sugar: 2 grams.

QUATTRO FORMAGGI PIZZA

- Total Cooking Time: 20-25 minutes
- Prep Time: 10 minutes
- Servings: 4

Ingredients:

- 1 pound (450g) pizza dough
- 1/2 cup grated mozzarella cheese
- 1/2 cup grated fontina cheese
- 1/2 cup grated gorgonzola cheese
- 1/2 cup grated Parmesan cheese
- 1 tablespoon extra virgin olive oil
- Freshly ground black pepper
- Fresh basil leaves (optional)

Directions:

1. To ensure optimal results, begin by preheating your oven to a temperature of 475°F (245°C). If you happen to possess a pizza stone, it is advisable to position it inside the oven as it preheats.
2. First, sprinkle some flour on a clean surface, then roll out the pizza dough to your preferred thickness. After completing the process of rolling out the dough, exercise caution when transferring it to either a parchment paper-lined baking sheet or, if available, a pizza peel when using a pizza stone.
3. To prepare the cheese mixture, combine the grated mozzarella, fontina, gorgonzola, and Parmesan cheeses in a bowl.
4. Evenly distribute the cheese mixture over the pizza dough, making sure to cover the edges. Gently pour a generous portion of extra virgin olive oil over the cheese, ensuring it is evenly coated. Sprinkle the cheese with freshly ground black pepper to add a touch of savory flavor.
5. Carefully transfer the pizza into the preheated oven. If using a baking sheet, place it directly on the oven rack. If you are using a pizza stone, carefully transfer the pizza onto the preheated stone.
6. You can bake the pizza in the oven for around 12 to 15 minutes, or until the crust achieves a lovely golden brown color and the cheese melts and develops a light brown hue.
7. Once the pizza is done baking, carefully remove it from the oven and let it cool for a short while. If you want to enhance the taste, feel free to decorate it with freshly plucked basil leaves for an added burst of flavor.

8. Slice the Quattro Formaggi pizza into desired portions and serve hot.

Nutritional breakdown per serving:

Calories: 350 kcal, Protein: 17 grams, Carbohydrates: 26 grams, Fat: 20 grams, Saturated Fat: 11 grams, Cholesterol: 50 milligrams, Sodium: 650 milligrams, Fiber: 2 grams, and Sugar: 1 grams.

PROSCIUTTO AND ARUGULA PIZZA

- Total Cooking Time: 15-20 minutes
- Prep Time: 10 minutes
- Servings: 4

Ingredients:

- 1 pound (450g) pizza dough
- 1/2 cup pizza sauce
- 1 cup shredded mozzarella cheese
- 4-6 slices of prosciutto
- 2 cups fresh arugula
- 1 tablespoon extra virgin olive oil
- Balsamic glaze (optional)
- Salt and pepper to taste

Directions:

1. To begin, set your oven to preheat at 475°F (245°C). If you happen to possess a pizza stone, go ahead and put it in the oven as it preheats.
2. On a surface dusted with flour, flatten the pizza dough to your preferred thickness. To ensure a smooth process, delicately transfer the flattened dough onto a baking sheet that has been prepped with parchment paper. In the case of using a pizza stone, carefully move the dough onto a pizza peel before proceeding to place it in the oven.
3. To begin, evenly distribute the pizza sauce across the dough, making sure to leave a small border around the edges. Afterwards, evenly distribute the shredded mozzarella cheese on top of the sauce to form a uniform layer.
4. Gently tear the prosciutto slices into smaller pieces and evenly scatter them over the layer of cheese.
5. Carefully transfer the pizza into the preheated oven. If using a baking sheet, place it directly on the oven rack. If you are utilizing a pizza stone, smoothly transfer the pizza onto the preheated stone by sliding it onto the surface.
6. You can let the pizza bake for around 10-12 minutes until the crust turns a lovely golden brown and the cheese is melted and irresistibly bubbly.
7. As the pizza bakes, take a bowl and gently combine the fresh arugula with extra virgin olive oil, salt, and pepper. Give the mixture a gentle toss to ensure all the ingredients are well combined.
8. Once you take the pizza out of the oven, let it cool for a few minutes before placing the dressed arugula on top as a delicious topping.
9. Drizzle with balsamic glaze, if desired, for added flavor.

10. Slice the Prosciutto and Arugula pizza into desired portions and serve hot.

Nutritional breakdown per serving:

Calories: 320 kcal, Protein: 15 grams, Carbohydrates: 38 grams, Fat: 12 grams, Saturated Fat: 5 grams, Cholesterol: 25 milligrams, Sodium: 800 milligrams, Fiber: 2 grams, and Sugar: 2 grams.

MEDITERRANEAN CHICKEN PIZZA

- Total Cooking Time: 25-30 minutes
- Prep Time: 15 minutes
- Servings: 4

Ingredients:

- 1 pound (450g) pizza dough
- 1/2 cup tomato sauce or pesto
- 1 cup cooked chicken, shredded or diced
- 1/2 cup sliced black olives
- 1/2 cup sliced cherry tomatoes
- 1/2 cup crumbled feta cheese
- 1/4 cup chopped red onion
- 1/4 cup chopped fresh basil
- 1 tablespoon extra virgin olive oil
- Salt and pepper to taste

Directions:

1. To get started, make sure to preheat your oven to the temperature specified for your pizza dough.
2. Flatten the pizza dough on a floured surface to achieve the thickness you desire. After completing the previous step, proceed to transfer the dough onto either a pizza stone or a baking sheet that has been properly prepared with parchment paper.
3. Evenly distribute the tomato sauce or pesto onto the dough, ensuring to leave a small border around the edges.
4. Sprinkle the cooked chicken breast, black olives, cherry tomatoes, feta cheese, red onion, and fresh basil over the sauce.
5. Gently pour the extra virgin olive oil over the toppings, and carefully season with salt and pepper according to personal preference.
6. Take caution as you move the pizza into the preheated oven and proceed to bake it based on the specific instructions for your pizza dough, typically for approximately 12-15 minutes or until the crust achieves a golden brown color and the cheese has melted and become bubbly.
7. Take the pizza out of the oven and allow it to cool for a few minutes before cutting it into slices.

Nutritional breakdown per serving:

Calories: 380 kcal, Protein: 23 grams, Carbohydrates: 38 grams, Fat: 15 grams, Saturated Fat: 4 grams, Cholesterol: 38 milligrams, Sodium: 780 milligrams, Fiber: 3 grams, and Sugar: 3 grams.

CAPRESE PIZZA

- Prep Time: 15 minutes
- Cooking Time: 15 minutes
- Total Time: 30 minutes
- Servings: 4

Ingredients:

- 1 pre-made pizza dough
- 1 cup cherry tomatoes, halved
- 8 ounces fresh mozzarella cheese, sliced
- 1/4 cup fresh basil leaves, torn
- 2 tablespoons extra-virgin olive oil
- 1 clove garlic, minced
- Salt and pepper to taste
- Balsamic glaze (optional)

Directions:

1. Before you start, make sure to preheat your oven to the temperature indicated on the pizza dough packaging.
2. Gently sprinkle some flour on a surface, and then roll out the pre-made pizza dough to achieve the desired shape and thickness.
3. Transfer the rolled-out dough onto a greased or parchment-lined baking sheet.
4. In a petite bowl, combine the finely chopped garlic with the olive oil. Apply the garlic-infused oil evenly onto the pizza dough, making sure to leave a narrow border around the edges.
5. Arrange the sliced mozzarella cheese evenly over the pizza dough.
6. Scatter the halved cherry tomatoes over the cheese, distributing them evenly.
7. Customize the flavor of the pizza by seasoning it with salt and pepper according to your personal taste preferences.
8. Once the pizza is in the preheated oven, adhere to the baking instructions provided on the pizza dough package. Alternatively, you can keep an eye on it until the crust achieves a delightful golden brown shade, and the cheese becomes irresistibly melted with enticing bubbles.
9. Once the pizza is out of the oven, sprinkle the torn basil leaves over the top.
10. Drizzle with balsamic glaze, if desired, for an extra burst of flavor.
11. Slice the Caprese pizza into wedges and serve hot.

Nutritional breakdown per serving:

Calories: 350 kcal, Protein: 15 grams, Carbohydrates: 30 grams, Fat: 18 grams, Saturated Fat: 8 grams, Cholesterol: 40 milligrams, Sodium: 650 milligrams, Fiber: 2 grams, and Sugar: 3 grams.

SPINACH AND FETA PIZZA

- Prep Time: 20 minutes
- Cooking Time: 15 minutes
- Total Time: 35 minutes
- Servings: 4

Ingredients:

- 1 pre-made pizza dough
- 2 cups fresh spinach leaves
- 4 ounces feta cheese, crumbled
- 1/4 cup diced red onion
- 1/4 cup sliced black olives
- 2 cloves garlic, minced
- 2 tablespoons olive oil
- 1 teaspoon dried oregano
- Salt and pepper to taste

Directions:

1. Set your oven to the temperature specified on the pizza dough package, allowing it to preheat.
2. Gently sprinkle some flour on a clean surface, then use a rolling pin to flatten the pre-made pizza dough to your desired thickness and shape.
3. Transfer the rolled-out dough onto a greased or parchment-lined baking sheet.
4. Preheat the frying pan to medium heat, then add the minced garlic and sauté until it becomes fragrant, typically around 1 minute.
5. Put the fresh spinach leaves in the skillet and cook them until they become wilted, which typically takes approximately 2-3 minutes. Once wilted, remove the skillet from heat and set it aside.
6. Apply the olive oil evenly onto the pizza dough, making sure to leave a small border around the edges.
7. Spread the wilted spinach evenly over the pizza dough.
8. Sprinkle the crumbled feta cheese, diced red onion, and sliced black olives over the spinach.
9. Season the pizza with dried oregano, salt, and pepper to taste.
10. Cook the pizza in the preheated oven as directed on the pizza dough package, or until the crust turns a golden brown and the cheese melts and lightly browns.
11. Once the pizza is out of the oven, let it cool for a few minutes before slicing.
12. Slice the Spinach and Feta pizza into wedges and serve hot.

Nutritional breakdown per serving:

Calories: 320 kcal, Protein: 10 grams, Carbohydrates: 30 grams, Fat: 18 grams, Saturated Fat: 6 grams, Cholesterol: 20 milligrams, Sodium: 760 milligrams, Fiber: 3 grams, and Sugar: 2 grams.

MEDITERRANEAN SEAFOOD PIZZA

- Prep Time: 20 minutes
- Cooking Time: 15-20 minutes
- Total Time: 35-40 minutes
- Servings: 4

Ingredients:

- 1 pre-made pizza dough
- 1/2 cup marinara sauce
- 8 ounces mixed seafood (shrimp, calamari, mussels), cooked and drained
- 1/4 cup sliced black olives
- 1/4 cup diced red onion
- 1/4 cup crumbled feta cheese
- 1/4 cup chopped fresh parsley
- 2 tablespoons extra-virgin olive oil
- 2 cloves garlic, minced
- Salt and pepper to taste

Directions:

1. Adjust your oven to the temperature indicated on the pizza dough package, and give it time to preheat.
2. Flatten the pre-made pizza dough on a floured surface to achieve the thickness and shape you desire.
3. Transfer the dough onto a greased or parchment-lined baking sheet.
4. In a compact bowl, combine the finely chopped garlic with the olive oil. Spread the garlic-infused oil evenly over the surface of the pizza dough, being careful to leave a small margin around the edges.
5. Distribute the marinara sauce evenly across the surface of the pizza dough.
6. Sprinkle the cooked seafood, sliced black olives, diced red onion, and crumbled feta cheese evenly on top of the sauce.
7. Add salt and pepper to the pizza according to your preferred taste.
8. Place the pizza in the oven that has been preheated, adhering to the guidelines provided on the pizza dough package, or until the crust achieves a delightful golden brown hue and the cheese becomes melted and lightly toasted.
9. Once the pizza is out of the oven, sprinkle the chopped fresh parsley over the top.
10. Let the pizza rest for a few minutes before cutting into it.
11. Slice the Mediterranean Seafood pizza into wedges and serve hot.

Nutritional breakdown per serving:

Calories: 425 kcal, Protein: 28 grams, Carbohydrates: 40 grams, Fat: 17 grams, Saturated Fat: 4 grams, Cholesterol: 135 milligrams, Sodium: 890 milligrams, Fiber: 2 grams, and Sugar: 3 grams.

MARGHERITA WITH A TWIST

- Prep Time: 15 minutes
- Cooking Time: 12-15 minutes
- Total Time: 27-30 minutes
- Servings: 4

Ingredients:

- 1 pre-made pizza dough
- 1/2 cup marinara sauce
- 8 ounces fresh mozzarella cheese, sliced
- 2 ripe tomatoes, thinly sliced
- 1/4 cup fresh basil leaves
- 2 tablespoons extra-virgin olive oil
- 2 cloves garlic, minced
- Salt and pepper to taste

Directions:

1. Adjust your oven to the temperature advised on the pizza dough package in order to preheat it.
2. Flatten the pre-made pizza dough on a floured surface to achieve the thickness and shape you prefer.
3. Transfer the dough onto a greased or parchment-lined baking sheet.
4. In a compact bowl, mix together the minced garlic and olive oil. Apply the garlic-infused oil evenly onto the pizza dough, ensuring to leave a small border around the edges.
5. Evenly distribute the marinara sauce across the surface of the pizza dough.
6. Place the sliced mozzarella cheese, tomato slices, and fresh basil leaves on the sauce, arranging them evenly.
7. Add salt and pepper to the pizza according to your taste preferences.
8. Prepare the pizza by baking it in the preheated oven following the instructions provided on the pizza dough package. Keep an eye on it until the crust achieves a delectable golden brown color and the cheese melts, acquiring a subtle hint of browning.
9. Once the pizza is out of the oven, let it cool for a few minutes before slicing.
10. Slice the Margherita pizza with a twist into wedges and serve hot.

Nutritional breakdown per serving:

Calories: 320 kcal, Protein: 14 grams, Carbohydrates: 30 grams, Fat: 16 grams, Saturated Fat: 7 grams, Cholesterol: 30 milligrams, Sodium: 650 milligrams, Fiber: 2 grams, and Sugar: 3 grams.

CHAPTER 2:
SEAFOOD PIZZA

SHRIMP SCAMPI PIZZA

- Prep Time: 15 minutes
- Cooking Time: 15-20 minutes
- Total Time: 30-35 minutes
- Servings: 4

Ingredients:

- 1 pre-made pizza dough
- 1/4 cup unsalted butter
- 4 cloves garlic, minced
- 1 pound medium shrimp, peeled and deveined
- 1/4 cup dry white wine
- 1/4 teaspoon crushed red pepper flakes
- Salt and pepper to taste
- 1 cup shredded mozzarella cheese
- 1/4 cup grated Parmesan cheese
- 2 tablespoons chopped fresh parsley

Directions:

1. Before you begin baking, ensure that the oven temperature aligns with the recommended setting mentioned on the pizza dough package.
2. On a floured surface, roll out the pre-made pizza dough to achieve the desired thickness and shape.
3. Transfer the dough onto a greased or parchment-lined baking sheet.
4. In a spacious skillet, melt the butter over medium heat. Introduce the minced garlic and cook it for approximately 1 minute until it becomes aromatic.
5. To cook the shrimp, simply add them to the skillet and cook them for a period of 2-3 minutes until they transform into a pink and opaque color.
6. Gently pour the white wine and lemon juice into the skillet, and delicately sprinkle in the crushed red pepper flakes (if you wish to add some heat). Let the mixture simmer for an extra 1 to 2 minutes, allowing the flavors to blend together in perfect harmony. Lastly, add a touch of salt and pepper to suit your personal taste preferences, ensuring a customized flavor profile.
7. Evenly distribute the shrimp scampi mixture onto the pizza dough, ensuring to leave a small space around the edges.
8. Generously scatter the shredded mozzarella cheese and grated Parmesan cheese on the surface.

9. Cook the pizza in the preheated oven as per the guidelines mentioned on the pizza dough package, or until the crust achieves a delightful golden brown color and the cheese is thoroughly melted with a slight browning.
10. Once the pizza is out of the oven, sprinkle the chopped fresh parsley over the top.
11. Let the pizza rest for a brief period to cool down before cutting into slices.
12. Slice the Shrimp Scampi pizza into wedges and serve hot.

Nutritional breakdown per serving:

Calories: 485 kcal, Protein: 35 grams, Carbohydrates: 31 grams, Fat: 24 grams, Saturated Fat: 14 grams, Cholesterol: 250 milligrams, Sodium: 670 milligrams, Fiber: 1 grams, and Sugar: 1 grams.

MEDITERRANEAN TUNA PIZZA

- Prep Time: 15 minutes
- Cooking Time: 12-15 minutes
- Total Time: 27-30 minutes
- Servings: 4

Ingredients:

- 1 pre-made pizza dough
- 1/4 cup tomato or marinara sauce
- 1 can (5 ounces) tuna, drained
- 1/2 cup sliced black olives
- 1/4 cup sliced red onions
- 1/4 cup sliced roasted red peppers
- 1/4 cup crumbled feta cheese
- 1 tablespoon chopped fresh basil
- 1 tablespoon chopped fresh parsley
- 2 tablespoons extra-virgin olive oil
- Salt and pepper to taste

Directions:

1. Heat up your oven to the temperature specified on the pizza dough package.
2. Using a floured surface, roll out the pre-made pizza dough to the thickness and shape you prefer.
3. Transfer the dough onto a greased or parchment-lined baking sheet.
4. Evenly distribute the tomato or marinara sauce over the pizza dough, making sure to leave a small border around the edges.
5. Flake the drained tuna over the sauce, distributing it evenly.
6. Sprinkle the sliced black olives, red onions, and roasted red peppers over the tuna.
7. Crumble the feta cheese over the top.
8. Drizzle the extra-virgin olive oil over the pizza.
9. Customize the flavor by incorporating salt and pepper to suit your personal taste preferences when adjusting the seasoning.
10. Cook the pizza in the preheated oven following the instructions on the pizza dough package, or until the crust turns a golden brown and the toppings are thoroughly heated.
11. Once the pizza is out of the oven, sprinkle the chopped fresh basil and parsley over the top.

12. Give the pizza a few minutes to cool down before you start slicing it.

Nutritional breakdown per serving:

Calories: 320 kcal, Protein: 16 grams, Carbohydrates: 32 grams, Fat: 14 grams, Saturated Fat: 3 grams, Cholesterol: 20 milligrams, Sodium: 780 milligrams, Fiber: 2 grams, and Sugar: 2 grams.

SEAFOOD MARINARA PIZZA

- Prep Time: 20 minutes
- Cooking Time: 15-20 minutes
- Total Time: 35-40 minutes
- Servings: 4

Ingredients:

- 1 pre-made pizza dough
- 1/2 cup marinara sauce
- 1/2 cup shredded mozzarella cheese
- 1/4 cup grated Parmesan cheese
- 1/4 cup sliced black olives
- 1/4 cup sliced red onions
- 1/4 cup sliced bell peppers
- 1/4 cup cooked shrimp, peeled and deveined
- 1/4 cup cooked scallops
- 1/4 cup cooked crab meat
- 1 tablespoon chopped fresh basil
- 1 tablespoon chopped fresh parsley
- 1 tablespoon extra-virgin olive oil
- Salt and pepper to taste

Directions:

1. To achieve the best possible outcome, it is essential to preheat your oven to the temperature specified on the pizza dough packaging before you begin cooking.
2. Start by taking the pre-made pizza dough and place it on a floured surface. Then, use a rolling pin to flatten and shape the dough according to your desired thickness and shape.
3. Transfer the dough onto a greased or parchment-lined baking sheet.
4. Carefully spread the marinara sauce in an even layer across the pizza dough, making sure to leave a small border around the edges for a balanced distribution.
5. Scatter the shredded mozzarella cheese and grated Parmesan cheese evenly over the sauce.
6. Arrange the sliced black olives, red onions, bell peppers, cooked shrimp, scallops, and crab meat over the cheese.
7. Drizzle the extra-virgin olive oil over the pizza.
8. Add salt and pepper according to your personal taste preferences.

9. Once the pizza is positioned inside the preheated oven, adhere to the instructions stated on the pizza dough package for the baking process. Maintain a vigilant watch over the pizza, ensuring that the crust achieves a desirable golden brown hue and the cheese is thoroughly melted and delicately browned.
10. Once the pizza is out of the oven, sprinkle the chopped fresh basil and parsley over the top.
11. To ensure easier slicing, it is recommended to let the pizza cool for a few minutes before cutting it into individual portions.

Nutritional breakdown per serving:

Calories: 380 kcal, Protein: 22 grams, Carbohydrates: 40 grams, Fat: 14 grams, Saturated Fat: 6 grams, Cholesterol: 85 milligrams, Sodium: 780 milligrams, Fiber: 2 grams, and Sugar: 3 grams.

SMOKED SALMON AND DILL PIZZA

- Prep Time: 15 minutes
- Cooking Time: 12-15 minutes
- Total Time: 27-30 minutes
- Servings: 4

Ingredients:

- 1 pre-made pizza dough
- 1/4 cup cream cheese
- 1/4 cup sour cream
- 1 tablespoon fresh dill, chopped
- 1/2 teaspoon lemon zest
- 1/4 teaspoon garlic powder
- Salt and pepper to taste
- 4 ounces smoked salmon, thinly sliced
- 1/4 cup red onion, thinly sliced
- 1/4 cup capers
- Fresh arugula for garnish

Directions:

1. Before placing the pizza in the oven, make sure to adjust the temperature to the recommended setting stated on the pizza dough package and ensure that the oven is preheated accordingly.
2. To achieve your preferred thickness and shape, gently roll out the pre-made pizza dough on a surface dusted with flour.
3. Transfer the dough onto a greased or parchment-lined baking sheet.
4. In a compact bowl, unite the cream cheese, sour cream, fresh dill, lemon zest, garlic powder, salt, and pepper. Mix the ingredients thoroughly until they are fully blended.
5. Evenly distribute the cream cheese mixture onto the pizza dough, ensuring to leave a narrow border around the edges.
6. Arrange the smoked salmon slices, red onion slices, and capers over the cream cheese mixture.
7. Place the pizza in the preheated oven and follow the instructions provided on the pizza dough package. Allow the pizza to bake until the crust achieves a delightful golden brown color and the toppings are completely heated.
8. Once the pizza is out of the oven, garnish with fresh arugula.
9. Give the pizza a few minutes to cool down before you start slicing it.

Nutritional breakdown per serving:

Calories: 244 320, Protein: 16 grams, Carbohydrates: 32 grams, Fat: 14 grams, Saturated Fat: 6 grams, Cholesterol: 40 milligrams, Sodium: 780 milligrams, Fiber: 2 grams, and Sugar: 2 grams.

ANCHOVY AND OLIVE PIZZA

- Prep Time: 15 minutes
- Cooking Time: 12-15 minutes
- Total Time: 27-30 minutes
- Servings: 4

Ingredients:

- 1 pre-made pizza dough
- 1/4 cup tomato sauce
- 1/4 cup sliced black olives
- 1/4 cup sliced green olives
- 4-6 anchovy fillets, rinsed and patted dry
- 2 tablespoons chopped fresh parsley
- 1 tablespoon extra-virgin olive oil
- 1/2 teaspoon dried oregano
- 1/4 teaspoon crushed red pepper flakes
- Salt and pepper to taste

Directions:

1. Before you start, it is important to ensure that your oven is preheated to the temperature specified on the pizza dough package.
2. Roll out the pre-made pizza dough on a surface dusted with flour, adjusting the thickness and shape to your preference.
3. Transfer the dough onto a greased or parchment-lined baking sheet.
4. Evenly distribute the tomato sauce over the pizza dough, ensuring to leave a narrow border around the edges.
5. Arrange the black olives and green olives over the sauce.
6. Place the anchovy fillets evenly over the olives.
7. Drizzle the extra-virgin olive oil over the pizza.
8. Generously sprinkle the freshly chopped parsley, dried oregano, optional crushed red pepper flakes, salt, and pepper over the surface of the pizza.
9. Carefully transfer the pizza into the preheated oven and bake it according to the instructions specified on the pizza dough package. Keep a close eye on it and remove it from the oven once the crust achieves a beautiful golden brown color and the toppings are thoroughly heated.
10. Once the pizza is out of the oven, allow it to cool for a few minutes before slicing.

Nutritional breakdown per serving:

Calories: 260 kcal, Protein: 9 grams, Carbohydrates: 33 grams, Fat: 10 grams, Saturated Fat: 2 grams, Cholesterol: 5 milligrams, Sodium: 900 milligrams, Fiber: 2 grams, and Sugar: 1 grams.

SCALLOP AND BACON PIZZA

- Prep Time: 20 minutes
- Cooking Time: 12-15 minutes
- Total Time: 32-35 minutes
- Servings: 4

Ingredients:

- 1 pre-made pizza dough
- 1/4 cup tomato sauce
- 1 cup shredded mozzarella cheese
- 4 slices bacon, cooked and crumbled
- 8-10 sea scallops, patted dry
- 1 tablespoon olive oil
- 2 cloves garlic, minced
- 1/4 teaspoon dried thyme
- Salt and pepper to taste
- Fresh parsley for garnish

Directions:

1. To get started, it is important to ensure that you preheat your oven to the temperature mentioned on the packaging of the pizza dough.
2. Flatten the pre-made pizza dough on a surface sprinkled with flour until it reaches the thickness and shape you desire.
3. Ensure that the tomato sauce is evenly spread over the pizza dough, being careful to leave a thin border around the edges.
4. To ensure even distribution, spread the tomato sauce evenly over the pizza dough, making sure to leave a small border around the edges.
5. Scatter the shredded mozzarella cheese on top of the sauce.
6. To begin, position a skillet on the stovetop over medium-high heat and warm up the olive oil. Next, introduce the minced garlic into the skillet and let it cook for about 1-2 minutes until it becomes aromatic, releasing a delightful fragrance.
7. Place the scallops into the skillet and cook them for approximately 1-2 minutes on each side until they achieve a light golden-brown color. Enhance their flavor by seasoning them with dried thyme, salt, and pepper.
8. Take the scallops out of the skillet and proceed to slice them into halves or quarters, adjusting the size based on their individual dimensions.
9. Arrange the bacon crumbles and sliced scallops evenly over the pizza.

10. To achieve a perfectly cooked pizza, place it in the preheated oven and follow the instructions on the pizza dough package. Continue baking the pizza until the crust achieves a delightful golden brown color and the toppings are thoroughly heated.
11. Once the pizza is out of the oven, garnish with fresh parsley.
12. It is recommended to let the pizza cool for a short period of time before slicing it.

Nutritional breakdown per serving:

Calories: 390 kcal, Protein: 20 grams, Carbohydrates: 33 grams, Fat: 19 grams, Saturated Fat: 7 grams, Cholesterol: 45 milligrams, Sodium: 910 milligrams, Fiber: 2 grams, and Sugar: 2 grams.

CLAM AND GARLIC PIZZA

- Prep Time: 20 minutes
- Cooking Time: 12-15 minutes
- Total Time: 32-35 minutes
- Servings: 4

Ingredients:

- 1 pre-made pizza dough
- 1/4 cup olive oil
- 4 cloves garlic, minced
- 1 cup shredded mozzarella cheese
- 1 cup canned minced clams, drained
- 1/4 cup chopped fresh parsley
- 1/2 teaspoon dried oregano
- Salt and pepper to taste
- Crushed red pepper flakes (optional)

Directions:

1. Prior to starting the cooking process, ensure that you preheat your oven to the specific temperature indicated on the pizza dough package.
2. Prepare a floured surface and gently roll out the pre-made pizza dough to achieve the thickness and shape that best suits your preferences.
3. Transfer the dough onto a greased or parchment-lined baking sheet.
4. To get started, warm the olive oil in a small saucepan over medium heat. Introduce the minced garlic and let it cook for 1-2 minutes until it releases a fragrant aroma. Take the saucepan off the heat and set it aside for future purposes.
5. Brush the garlic-infused olive oil over the pizza dough, ensuring an even coating.
6. Evenly distribute the shredded mozzarella cheese on top of the olive oil infused with garlic.
7. Spread the minced clams evenly over the pizza.
8. Sprinkle the chopped fresh parsley, dried oregano, salt, pepper, and crushed red pepper flakes (if desired) over the top.
9. Cook the pizza in the preheated oven following the instructions provided on the pizza dough package, or until the crust achieves a golden brown color and the toppings are thoroughly heated.
10. Once the pizza is out of the oven, allow it to cool for a few minutes before slicing.

Nutritional breakdown per serving:

Calories: 350 kcal, Protein: 16 grams, Carbohydrates: 32 grams, Fat: 18 grams, Saturated Fat: 4 grams, Cholesterol: 30 milligrams, Sodium: 780 milligrams, Fiber: 2 grams, and Sugar: 2 grams.

LOBSTER AND SPINACH PIZZA

- Prep Time: 25 minutes
- Cooking Time: 12-15 minutes
- Total Time: 37-40 minutes
- Servings: 4

Ingredients:

- 1 pre-made pizza dough
- 1/4 cup tomato sauce
- 1 cup shredded mozzarella cheese
- 1/2 cup cooked lobster meat, chopped
- 1 cup baby spinach leaves
- 1/4 cup sliced red onion
- 2 cloves garlic, minced
- 1 tablespoon olive oil
- 1/4 teaspoon dried basil
- Salt and pepper to taste
- Fresh basil leaves for garnish

Directions:

1. To ensure the desired result, it is crucial to preheat your oven to the temperature specified on the pizza dough package before you start cooking. This particular step is essential in attaining the ideal texture and flavor profile for your pizza.
2. Use a floured surface to roll out the pre-made pizza dough until it reaches the desired thickness and shape.
3. Transfer the dough onto a greased or parchment-lined baking sheet.
4. Evenly distribute the tomato sauce over the pizza dough, making sure to leave a small border around the edges.
5. Distribute the shredded mozzarella cheese evenly across the sauce.
6. Begin by heating the skillet on medium-high heat and adding the olive oil. Once the oil is hot, incorporate the minced garlic and cook it for approximately 1-2 minutes until it emits a fragrant aroma.
7. Add the baby spinach leaves to the skillet and cook for 2-3 minutes until wilted. Season with dried basil, salt, and pepper.
8. Spread the cooked spinach evenly over the pizza.
9. Scatter the chopped lobster meat and sliced red onion over the pizza.

10. Follow the instructions provided on the pizza dough package and bake the pizza in the preheated oven until the crust achieves a golden brown color and the toppings are thoroughly heated.
11. Once the pizza is out of the oven, garnish with fresh basil leaves.
12. Before slicing, give the pizza a few minutes to cool down.

Nutritional breakdown per serving:

Calories: 380 kcal, Protein: 22 grams, Carbohydrates: 37 grams, Fat: 16 grams, Saturated Fat: 6 grams, Cholesterol: 65 milligrams, Sodium: 780 milligrams, Fiber: 2 grams, and Sugar: 3 grams.

MEDITERRANEAN CRAB PIZZA

- Prep Time: 20 minutes
- Cooking Time: 12-15 minutes
- Total Time: 32-35 minutes
- Servings: 4

Ingredients:

- 1 pre-made pizza dough
- 1/4 cup tomato sauce
- 1 cup shredded mozzarella cheese
- 1 cup lump crab meat
- 1/4 cup sliced Kalamata olives
- 1/4 cup sliced sun-dried tomatoes
- 1/4 cup crumbled feta cheese
- 2 tablespoons chopped fresh basil
- 2 tablespoons chopped fresh parsley
- 1 tablespoon olive oil
- 2 cloves garlic, minced
- Salt and pepper to taste
- Lemon wedges for serving (optional)

Directions:

1. Set your oven to the temperature suggested on the pizza dough package to preheat it.
2. Take the pre-made pizza dough and roll it out on a floured surface to achieve your desired thickness and shape.
3. Make certain that the tomato sauce is evenly spread on the pizza dough, ensuring a small border is left around the edges.
4. Apply the tomato sauce in a uniform manner on the pizza dough, ensuring to leave a small gap along the edges.
5. Distribute the shredded mozzarella cheese evenly across the sauce.
6. Using a skillet, warm the olive oil over medium heat. Add the minced garlic and sauté for 1-2 minutes until it becomes fragrant.
7. Introduce the lump crab meat into the skillet and cook for 2-3 minutes until it is heated thoroughly. Enhance the overall taste experience by incorporating a subtle blend of salt and pepper, resulting in a heightened flavor profile.
8. Spread the cooked crab meat evenly over the pizza.
9. Scatter the sliced Kalamata olives and sun-dried tomatoes over the pizza.

10. Sprinkle the crumbled feta cheese, chopped fresh basil, and chopped fresh parsley over the top.
11. Cook the pizza in the preheated oven following the guidelines provided on the pizza dough packaging, or until the crust turns a golden brown and the toppings are thoroughly heated.
12. If desired, after removing the pizza from the oven, you can opt to drizzle it with freshly squeezed lemon juice.
13. Before slicing, give the pizza a few minutes to cool down.

Nutritional breakdown per serving:

Calories: 420 kcal, Protein: 24 grams, Carbohydrates: 42 grams, Fat: 18 grams, Saturated Fat: 6 grams, Cholesterol: 80 milligrams, Sodium: 980 milligrams, Fiber: 2 grams, and Sugar: 3 grams.

MIXED SEAFOOD AND PESTO PIZZA

- Prep Time: 20 minutes
- Cooking Time: 15 minutes
- Total Time: 35 minutes
- Servings: 4

Ingredients:

- 1 prepared pizza dough
- 1/4 cup store-bought pesto sauce
- 1 cup mixed seafood (shrimp, squid, and mussels)
- 1/2 cup cherry tomatoes, halved
- 1/4 cup sliced black olives
- 1/4 cup sliced red onions
- 1 cup shredded mozzarella cheese
- Fresh basil leaves, for garnish
- Salt and pepper to taste

Directions:

1. To get started, set your oven to a temperature of 450°F (230°C) and make sure to place a pizza stone or baking sheet inside to ensure that it gets heated up along with the oven.
2. To achieve your desired thickness, roll out the pizza dough you have prepared on a surface that has been lightly dusted with flour. Then, carefully transfer the rolled-out dough onto a sheet of parchment paper.
3. To ensure even distribution, spread the pesto sauce evenly across the pizza dough, leaving a small border around the edges.
4. To cook the mixed seafood thoroughly, heat a skillet over medium heat and sauté the seafood for approximately 3-4 minutes. Remember to season with salt and pepper according to your taste preferences.
5. Arrange the cooked seafood, cherry tomatoes, black olives, and red onions evenly over the pesto sauce.
6. Distribute the shredded mozzarella cheese evenly across the toppings.
7. To safely move the pizza from the parchment paper to the heated pizza stone or baking sheet in the oven, handle it with care and attention. This will guarantee that the pizza moves securely without any mishaps.
8. You should let the pizza bake for around 12-15 minutes, or until the crust turns a beautiful golden brown and the cheese becomes melted and bubbly.

9. Remove from the oven and let the pizza cool for a few minutes. Garnish with fresh basil leaves.
10. Slice the pizza into desired portions and serve hot.

Nutritional breakdown per serving:

Calories: 350 kcal, Protein: 22 grams, Carbohydrates: 30 grams, Fat: 15 grams, Saturated Fat: 6 grams, Cholesterol: 75 milligrams, Sodium: 600 milligrams, Fiber: 2 grams, and Sugar: 2 grams.

CHAPTER 3: VEGITERANEAN PIZZA

MARGHERITA PIZZA

- Prep Time: 15 minutes
- Cooking Time: 12-15 minutes
- Total Time: 27-30 minutes
- Servings: 4

Ingredients:

- 1 prepared pizza dough
- 1/4 cup extra virgin olive oil
- 2 cloves garlic, minced
- 4 large tomatoes, sliced
- 8 ounces fresh mozzarella cheese, sliced
- Fresh basil leaves
- Salt and pepper to taste

Directions:

1. Prior to beginning, ensure that the oven is preheated to 475°F (245°C) and that a pizza stone or baking sheet is placed inside to become hot.
2. Take a small bowl and mix together the extra virgin olive oil and minced garlic, then set the mixture aside for later use.
3. To attain the desired thickness, flatten the prepared pizza dough on a surface dusted with a light layer of flour. Next, gently transfer the dough onto a sheet of parchment paper.
4. Apply the garlic-infused olive oil evenly onto the pizza dough, ensuring to leave a small margin around the edges.
5. Arrange the sliced tomatoes evenly over the olive oil.
6. Position the fresh mozzarella cheese slices on top of the tomatoes in an organized manner.
7. Add salt and pepper according to your preferred taste preferences.
8. When transferring the pizza and parchment paper to the preheated pizza stone or baking sheet inside the oven, it is vital to handle them with care and caution. Ensuring the pizza is handled carefully helps reduce the chances of accidents or mishaps.
9. Place the pizza inside the oven and allow it to bake for approximately 12 to 15 minutes, or until the crust takes on a delightful golden brown hue, while the cheese achieves a state of complete melting and begins to bubble enticingly.
10. Remove from the oven and let the pizza cool for a few minutes. Garnish with fresh basil leaves.
11. Slice the pizza into desired portions and serve hot.

Nutritional breakdown per serving:

Calories: 350 kcal, Protein: 15 grams, Carbohydrates: 30 grams, Fat: 20 grams, Saturated Fat: 8 grams, Cholesterol: 25 milligrams, Sodium: 500 milligrams, Fiber: 2 grams, and Sugar: 4 grams.

MEDITERRANEAN VEGGIE PIZZA

- Prep Time: 20 minutes
- Cooking Time: 15 minutes
- Total Time: 35 minutes
- Servings: 4

Ingredients:

- 1 prepared pizza dough
- 1/4 cup tomato sauce
- 2 tablespoons olive oil
- 2 cloves garlic, minced
- 1/2 teaspoon dried oregano
- 1/4 teaspoon red pepper flakes (optional)
- 1/2 cup sliced red bell pepper
- 1/2 cup sliced yellow bell pepper
- 1/2 cup sliced red onion
- 1/2 cup sliced black olives
- 1/2 cup crumbled feta cheese
- 1/4 cup chopped fresh basil
- Salt and pepper to taste

Directions:

1. To begin, set the oven temperature to 450°F (230°C) and wait for it to preheat. Next, position a pizza stone or baking sheet inside the oven to heat up alongside.
2. Take a small bowl and mix together tomato sauce, olive oil, minced garlic, dried oregano, and red pepper flakes (if desired). Keep the mixture aside for later use.
3. On a surface dusted with a light layer of flour, flatten the prepared pizza dough to your preferred thickness. Then, carefully move the dough onto a sheet of parchment paper.
4. Ensure that the tomato sauce mixture is spread evenly over the pizza dough, while also leaving a narrow border around the edges to maintain a defined crust.
5. Arrange the sliced red and yellow bell peppers, red onion, and black olives evenly over the sauce.
6. Distribute the crumbled feta cheese evenly over the toppings, ensuring that it covers the entire surface.
7. Customize the flavor to suit your liking by incorporating salt and pepper according to your taste.

8. It is essential to be cautious and handle the pizza and parchment paper carefully when placing them onto the preheated pizza stone or baking sheet in the oven, ensuring that they are properly positioned.
9. Bake for a duration of 12-15 minutes, or until the crust achieves a golden brown color and the cheese is melted and forms bubbles.
10. Remove from the oven and let the pizza cool for a few minutes. Sprinkle fresh basil over the top.
11. Slice the pizza into desired portions and serve hot.

Nutritional breakdown per serving:

Calories: 330 kcal, Protein: 10 grams, Carbohydrates: 38 grams, Fat: 15 grams, Saturated Fat: 5 grams, Cholesterol: 20 milligrams, Sodium: 600 milligrams, Fiber: 3 grams, and Sugar: 4 grams.

ROASTED VEGETABLE PIZZA

- Prep Time: 20 minutes
- Cooking Time: 25 minutes
- Total Time: 45 minutes
- Servings: 4

Ingredients:

- 1 prepared pizza dough
- 1/4 cup tomato sauce
- 2 tablespoons olive oil
- 2 cloves garlic, minced
- 1/2 teaspoon dried oregano
- 1/4 teaspoon red pepper flakes (optional)
- 1 cup sliced bell peppers (assorted colors)
- 1 cup sliced zucchini
- 1 cup sliced red onion
- 1 cup sliced mushrooms
- 1/2 cup shredded mozzarella cheese
- 1/4 cup grated Parmesan cheese
- Fresh basil leaves for garnish
- Salt and pepper to taste

Directions:

1. First and foremost, make sure that your oven is preheated to a temperature of 450°F (230°C). Following that, carefully place either a pizza stone or a baking sheet inside the oven, allowing it to heat up thoroughly.
2. Take a small bowl and combine tomato sauce, olive oil, minced garlic, dried oregano, and red pepper flakes (if preferred). Set the mixture aside to be used later.
3. Flatten the prepared pizza dough on a surface sprinkled with a small amount of flour until it reaches your preferred thickness. Then, carefully move the dough onto a sheet of parchment paper.
4. Evenly distribute the tomato sauce mixture over the pizza dough, making sure to leave a thin border around the edges.
5. Arrange the sliced bell peppers, zucchini, red onion, and mushrooms evenly over the sauce.
6. Scatter the shredded mozzarella cheese and grated Parmesan cheese evenly over the toppings.

7. Customize the flavor to suit your liking by incorporating salt and pepper according to your taste.
8. When transferring the pizza onto the preheated pizza stone or baking sheet in the oven, it is important to exercise caution and handle the process with care. Make sure to be precise and ensure a smooth transfer, taking extra care with the parchment paper.
9. The recommended baking time for achieving a golden brown crust and melted, bubbly cheese is 20-25 minutes.
10. Remove from the oven and let the pizza cool for a few minutes. Garnish with fresh basil leaves.
11. Slice the pizza into desired portions and serve hot.

Nutritional breakdown per serving:

Calories: 280 kcal, Protein: 9 grams, Carbohydrates: 38 grams, Fat: 10 grams, Saturated Fat: 3 grams, Cholesterol: 10 milligrams, Sodium: 500 milligrams, Fiber: 4 grams, and Sugar: 5 grams.

GREEK PIZZA

- Prep Time: 20 minutes
- Cooking Time: 15 minutes
- Total Time: 35 minutes
- Servings: 4

Ingredients:

- 1 prepared pizza dough
- 1/4 cup tomato sauce
- 2 tablespoons olive oil
- 2 cloves garlic, minced
- 1/2 teaspoon dried oregano
- 1/4 teaspoon red pepper flakes (optional)
- 1 cup sliced cherry tomatoes
- 1/2 cup sliced Kalamata olives
- 1/2 cup sliced red onion
- 1/2 cup crumbled feta cheese
- 1/4 cup chopped fresh parsley
- Salt and pepper to taste

Directions:

1. To prepare the oven for cooking, here are the steps to follow: Start by setting the temperature to 450°F (230°C) and allowing it to preheat. Next, place a pizza stone or baking sheet inside the oven to ensure that it also heats up properly.
2. To prepare the sauce, combine tomato sauce, olive oil, minced garlic, dried oregano, and red pepper flakes (if preferred) in a small bowl. Set the mixture aside for future use.
3. To achieve your desired thickness, roll out the pizza dough on a surface lightly dusted with flour. Once rolled, carefully transfer the dough onto a sheet of parchment paper.
4. To evenly distribute the tomato sauce mixture, spread it over the pizza dough, ensuring to leave a small border around the edges.
5. Arrange the sliced cherry tomatoes, Kalamata olives, and red onion evenly over the sauce.
6. Sprinkle the crumbled feta cheese over the toppings.
7. To achieve the desired flavor, modify the taste according to your personal preference by adding salt and pepper.

8. To ensure a safe transition of the pizza from the parchment paper to the preheated pizza stone or baking sheet in the oven, it is important to handle it with care and exercise caution.
9. Allow the pizza to bake for approximately 12-15 minutes, or until the crust achieves a lovely golden brown hue and the cheese becomes irresistibly melted and bubbly.
10. Remove from the oven and let the pizza cool for a few minutes. Sprinkle fresh parsley over the top.
11. Slice the pizza into desired portions and serve hot.

Nutritional breakdown per serving:

Calories: 340 kcal, Protein: 12 grams, Carbohydrates: 36 grams, Fat: 17 grams, Saturated Fat: 6 grams, Cholesterol: 25 milligrams, Sodium: 670 milligrams, Fiber: 3 grams, and Sugar: 5 grams.

SPINACH AND FETA PIZZA

- Prep Time: 15 minutes
- Cooking Time: 15 minutes
- Total Time: 30 minutes
- Servings: 4

Ingredients:

- 1 prepared pizza dough
- 1/4 cup tomato sauce
- 2 tablespoons olive oil
- 2 cloves garlic, minced
- 2 cups fresh spinach leaves
- 1 cup crumbled feta cheese
- 1/2 cup sliced black olives
- 1/4 cup sliced red onion
- 1/2 teaspoon dried oregano
- Salt and pepper to taste

Directions:

1. To achieve a temperature of 450°F (230°C), preheat the oven beforehand. Once the oven is heated, carefully place a pizza stone or baking sheet inside to allow it to heat up as well.
2. To start, combine tomato sauce, olive oil, and minced garlic in a small bowl. Set the mixture aside for future use.
3. Flatten the prepared pizza dough on a surface dusted with a small amount of flour until it reaches the desired thickness. Position the dough onto a piece of parchment paper.
4. Evenly distribute the tomato sauce mixture over the pizza dough, making sure to leave a small border around the edges.
5. Arrange the fresh spinach leaves evenly over the sauce.
6. Sprinkle the crumbled feta cheese, sliced black olives, and sliced red onion over the toppings.
7. Add a desired amount of dried oregano, salt, and pepper for seasoning.
8. To guarantee a safe cooking experience, it is strongly advised to handle the pizza with caution during the transfer from the parchment paper to the preheated pizza stone or baking sheet in the oven.

9. To prepare the dish, carefully position it in the oven and allow it to bake for roughly 12-15 minutes, or until the crust reaches a desirable golden brown hue and the cheese is thoroughly melted and bubbling.
10. Remove from the oven and let the pizza cool for a few minutes.
11. Slice the pizza into desired portions and serve hot.

Nutritional breakdown per serving:

Calories: 280 kcal, Protein: 10 grams, Carbohydrates: 32 grams, Fat: 12 grams, Saturated Fat: 5 grams, Cholesterol: 25 milligrams, Sodium: 650 milligrams, Fiber: 2 grams, and Sugar: 2 grams.

CAPRESE PIZZA

- Prep Time: 15 minutes
- Cooking Time: 15 minutes
- Total Time: 30 minutes
- Servings: 4

Ingredients:

- 1 prepared pizza dough
- 1/4 cup tomato sauce
- 2 tablespoons olive oil
- 2 cloves garlic, minced
- 2 large tomatoes, sliced
- 8 ounces fresh mozzarella cheese, sliced
- 1/2 cup fresh basil leaves
- Balsamic glaze, for drizzling
- Salt and pepper to taste

Directions:

1. For preparation, adjust the oven temperature to 450°F (230°C) and place either a pizza stone or a baking sheet inside with care, allowing it to preheat.
2. Combine tomato sauce, olive oil, and minced garlic in a small bowl. Set it aside for later use.
3. Use a lightly floured surface to roll out the prepared pizza dough to your preferred thickness. Then, carefully transfer the dough onto a sheet of parchment paper.
4. Evenly distribute the tomato sauce mixture across the pizza dough, ensuring to leave a small border around the edges.
5. Arrange the sliced tomatoes evenly over the sauce.
6. Place the fresh mozzarella slices on top of the tomatoes.
7. Gently tear the fresh basil leaves into smaller pieces and sprinkle them over the pizza.
8. To achieve the desired flavor, modify the taste according to your personal preference by adding salt and pepper.
9. When transferring the pizza and parchment paper to the preheated pizza stone or baking sheet inside the oven, it is vital to handle them with care and caution. Ensuring the pizza is handled carefully helps reduce the chances of accidents or mishaps.
10. Bake the pizza for around 12 to 15 minutes, or until the crust achieves a delightful golden brown hue and the cheese is wonderfully melted and bubbly.
11. Remove from the oven and let the pizza cool for a few minutes.
12. Drizzle balsamic glaze over the top of the pizza.

13. Slice the pizza into desired portions and serve hot.

Nutritional breakdown per serving:

Calories: 350 kcal, Protein: 16 grams, Carbohydrates: 30 grams, Fat: 18 grams, Saturated Fat: 8 grams, Cholesterol: 40 milligrams, Sodium: 600 milligrams, Fiber: 2 grams, and Sugar: 4 grams.

MEDITERRANEAN PESTO PIZZA

- Prep Time: 15 minutes
- Cooking Time: 15 minutes
- Total Time: 30 minutes
- Servings: 4

Ingredients:

- 1 prepared pizza dough
- 1/4 cup pesto sauce
- 2 tablespoons olive oil
- 2 cloves garlic, minced
- 1 cup cherry tomatoes, halved
- 1/2 cup sliced black olives
- 1/4 cup sliced red onion
- 1/2 cup crumbled feta cheese
- 1/4 cup chopped fresh basil leaves
- Salt and pepper to taste

Directions:

1. To initiate the cooking procedure, it is important to ensure that the oven is preheated to a temperature of 450°F (230°C). Following that, exercise caution while positioning a pizza stone or baking sheet inside the oven to ensure proper heating.
2. Combine pesto sauce, olive oil, and minced garlic in a small bowl. Set it aside for future use.
3. On a surface lightly dusted with flour, use a rolling pin to flatten the prepared pizza dough to your preferred thickness. Then, carefully transfer the rolled-out dough onto a sheet of parchment paper.
4. Apply the pesto sauce mixture evenly onto the pizza dough, ensuring to leave a small border around the edges.
5. Arrange the cherry tomatoes, black olives, and red onion slices evenly over the sauce.
6. Sprinkle the crumbled feta cheese and chopped fresh basil leaves over the toppings.
7. Personalize the flavor to your liking by incorporating salt and pepper to achieve the desired taste that aligns with your individual preferences.
8. When transferring the pizza and parchment paper to the preheated pizza stone or baking sheet inside the oven, it is vital to handle them with care and caution. Ensuring the pizza is handled carefully helps reduce the chances of accidents or mishaps.
9. Cook for a duration of 12-15 minutes, or until the crust achieves a golden brown color and the cheese is thoroughly melted and bubbling.

10. Remove from the oven and let the pizza cool for a few minutes.
11. Slice the pizza into desired portions and serve hot.

Nutritional breakdown per serving:

Calories: 320 kcal, Protein: 10 grams, Carbohydrates: 32 grams, Fat: 18 grams, Saturated Fat: 5 grams, Cholesterol: 15 milligrams, Sodium: 650 milligrams, Fiber: 2 grams, and Sugar: 3 grams.

HUMMUS AND ROASTED RED PEPPER PIZZA

- Prep Time: 15 minutes
- Cooking Time: 15 minutes
- Total Time: 30 minutes
- Servings: 4

Ingredients:

- 1 prepared pizza dough
- 1/2 cup hummus
- 1/4 cup roasted red pepper strips
- 1/4 cup sliced black olives
- 1/4 cup crumbled feta cheese
- 2 tablespoons chopped fresh parsley
- Salt and pepper to taste

Directions:

1. To begin, adjust the oven temperature to 450°F (230°C) and give it time to preheat. Then, place a pizza stone or baking sheet inside the oven to warm up.
2. Begin by rolling out the pizza dough that has been prepared on a surface that has been lightly dusted with flour, until it is at the thickness you desire. After that, transfer the rolled-out dough onto a sheet of parchment paper.
3. Ensure that the hummus is spread evenly across the pizza dough, making sure to leave a small border around the edges.
4. Arrange the roasted red pepper strips and black olives evenly over the hummus.
5. Sprinkle the crumbled feta cheese and chopped fresh parsley over the toppings.
6. Customize the flavor by adding salt and pepper to your liking.
7. To ensure safety and prevent accidents or mishaps, it is important to handle the pizza, along with the parchment paper, with care when transferring it onto the preheated pizza stone or baking sheet that is already in the oven.
8. To ensure optimal cooking, preheat the oven and carefully position the dish inside. Allow it to bake for a duration of roughly 12-15 minutes, or until the crust achieves a delightful golden brown hue and the cheese reaches a state of complete melting, with tiny bubbles forming on its surface.
9. Remove from the oven and let the pizza cool for a few minutes.
10. Slice the pizza into desired portions and serve hot.

Nutritional breakdown per serving:

Calories: 280 kcal, Protein: 9 grams, Carbohydrates: 38 grams, Fat: 10 grams, Saturated Fat: 2 grams, Cholesterol: 5 milligrams, Sodium: 680 milligrams, Fiber: 4 grams, and Sugar: 2 grams.

CARAMELIZED ONION AND GOAT CHEESE PIZZA

- Prep Time: 15 minutes
- Cooking Time: 45 minutes
- Total Time: 1 hour
- Servings: 4

Ingredients:

- 1 prepared pizza dough
- 2 large onions, thinly sliced
- 2 tablespoons olive oil
- 1 tablespoon balsamic vinegar
- 1 teaspoon sugar
- 4 ounces goat cheese, crumbled
- 2 tablespoons chopped fresh thyme
- Salt and pepper to taste

Directions:

1. Begin by setting the oven temperature to 425°F (220°C) and allowing it to preheat. Simultaneously, you can place a pizza stone or baking sheet inside the oven to preheat alongside.
2. Choose a big skillet and warm some olive oil over medium heat. Add the sliced onions and cook them, stirring occasionally, until they turn soft and caramelized, which usually takes around 20 to 25 minutes.
3. Blend the balsamic vinegar and sugar into the mixture, then cook for an additional 5 minutes until the onions turn dark and caramelized. Take the skillet off the heat and place it aside.
4. Take the pizza dough and gently roll it out on a floured surface, adjusting the thickness to your liking. Then, carefully transfer the dough onto a sheet of parchment paper.
5. Ensure the caramelized onions are spread evenly over the entire surface of the pizza dough, leaving a thin border around the edges for a balanced distribution.
6. Sprinkle the crumbled goat cheese and chopped fresh thyme over the onions.
7. Customize the flavor by adding salt and pepper to your liking.
8. To prevent accidents or mishaps, it is important to handle the pizza, along with the parchment paper, with caution when placing it onto the preheated pizza stone or baking sheet inside the oven.

9. To cook the dish, put it inside the oven and bake it for a duration of 15 to 20 minutes. Keep an eye on it and remove it when the crust turns a delightful golden brown, and the cheese has melted and acquired a light brown color.
10. Remove from the oven and let the pizza cool for a few minutes.
11. Slice the pizza into desired portions and serve hot.

Nutritional breakdown per serving:

Calories: 320 kcal, Protein: 10 grams, Carbohydrates: 40 grams, Fat: 14 grams, Saturated Fat: 6 grams, Cholesterol: 15 milligrams, Sodium: 380 milligrams, Fiber: 3 grams, and Sugar: 8 grams.

MUSHROOM AND TRUFFLE PIZZA

- Prep Time: 20 minutes
- Cooking Time: 25 minutes
- Total Time: 45 minutes
- Servings: 4

Ingredients:

- 1 prepared pizza dough
- 1 tablespoon olive oil
- 8 ounces sliced mushrooms
- 2 cloves garlic, minced
- 2 tablespoons truffle oil
- 1 cup shredded mozzarella cheese
- 1/4 cup grated Parmesan cheese
- Fresh thyme leaves for garnish
- Salt and pepper to taste

Directions:

1. Before you start cooking, it is advisable to preheat your oven to a temperature of 450°F (230°C). As the oven starts to preheat, you can put either a pizza stone or a baking sheet inside to allow it to heat up simultaneously with the oven.
2. To warm the olive oil, simply place a large frying pan on the stove and set the heat to medium. Cook the sliced mushrooms and minced garlic until they become tender and lightly browned, typically within 5-7 minutes. Season with salt and pepper as desired. Remove from heat and set aside.
3. To achieve the desired thickness, roll out the prepared pizza dough on a surface lightly dusted with flour. Then, carefully transfer the dough to a sheet of parchment paper.
4. Evenly distribute the truffle oil over the pizza dough, making sure to leave a small border around the edges.
5. Spread the sautéed mushrooms and garlic mixture evenly over the truffle oil.
6. Evenly distribute the shredded mozzarella cheese and grated Parmesan cheese over the toppings.
7. To enhance the flavors, add salt and pepper according to your preference, ensuring that the dish is seasoned to your liking.
8. Handle the pizza transfer onto the preheated pizza stone or baking sheet with caution to ensure safety. Stay attentive and careful to avoid any accidents or mishaps.

9. Place the pizza in the oven and bake it for approximately 12-15 minutes, or until the crust turns a delightful golden brown and the cheese is melted and starts to bubble.
10. Remove from the oven and let the pizza cool for a few minutes.
11. Garnish with fresh thyme leaves before serving.

Nutritional breakdown per serving:

Calories: 320 kcal, Protein: 14 grams, Carbohydrates: 25 grams, Fat: 18 grams, Saturated Fat: 6 grams, Cholesterol: 25 milligrams, Sodium: 580 milligrams, Fiber: 2 grams, and Sugar: 2 grams.

CHAPTER 4: CREATIVE AND UNIQUE PIZZA COMBINATIONS

FIG AND PROSCIUTTO PIZZA

- Prep Time: 15 minutes
- Cooking Time: 15 minutes
- Total Time: 30 minutes
- Servings: 4

Ingredients:

- 1 prepared pizza dough
- 1/4 cup fig jam
- 4 ounces fresh mozzarella cheese, sliced
- 4 slices prosciutto
- 4 fresh figs, sliced
- 1 cup arugula
- Balsamic glaze, for drizzling
- Salt and pepper to taste

Directions:

1. Prior to starting, make sure to preheat the oven to 450°F (230°C). Then, place a pizza stone or baking sheet inside and let it heat up.
2. Gently flatten the pizza dough that has been prepared onto a surface dusted with flour until it reaches your desired thickness. Subsequently, carefully move the dough onto a sheet of parchment paper.
3. Ensure that you spread the fig jam evenly across the pizza dough, taking care to leave a small border around the edges.
4. Place the sliced mozzarella cheese on the surface of the fig jam, ensuring it is evenly arranged.
5. Tear the prosciutto into smaller pieces and distribute them over the cheese.
6. Place the fresh fig slices on the pizza.
7. To enhance flavor, adjust salt and pepper to your taste preferences for a delightful culinary experience.
8. Carefully position the pizza on the hot pizza stone or baking sheet in the oven, using the parchment paper as a foundation, ensuring gentle handling.
9. Place the pizza in the oven and bake for around 12 to 15 minutes, or until the crust turns a delightful golden brown and the cheese is melted and bubbling irresistibly.
10. Remove from the oven and let the pizza cool for a few minutes.
11. Finish off the dish by adding a generous amount of fresh arugula on top and giving it a delightful drizzle of balsamic glaze.
12. Slice the pizza into desired portions and serve hot.

Nutritional breakdown per serving:

Calories: 330 kcal, Protein: 16 grams, Carbohydrates: 36 grams, Fat: 14 grams, Saturated Fat: 6 grams, Cholesterol: 25 milligrams, Sodium: 580 milligrams, Fiber: 2 grams, and Sugar: 15 grams.

MEDITERRANEAN BREAKFAST PIZZA

- Prep Time: 15 minutes
- Cooking Time: 20 minutes
- Total Time: 35 minutes
- Servings: 4

Ingredients:

- 1 prepared pizza dough
- 4 large eggs
- 1/4 cup sun-dried tomato pesto
- 1/2 cup crumbled feta cheese
- 1/2 cup sliced Kalamata olives
- 1/4 cup chopped fresh basil
- 1/4 cup chopped roasted red peppers
- Salt and pepper to taste

Directions:

1. To ensure optimal results, it is important to preheat the oven to a temperature of 450°F (230°C) before beginning. Position a pizza stone or baking sheet inside the oven and allow it to heat up thoroughly.
2. Begin by rolling out the pizza dough that you have prepared on a surface that has been lightly dusted with flour, ensuring that it reaches the thickness you desire. Once done, gently transfer the dough onto a sheet of parchment paper.
3. Evenly spread the sun-dried tomato pesto on the pizza dough, leaving a small border along the edges.
4. Sprinkle the crumbled feta cheese over the pesto.
5. Arrange the sliced Kalamata olives, chopped fresh basil, and roasted red peppers on top of the cheese.
6. Create four wells in the toppings and crack an egg into each well.
7. To enhance flavor, adjust salt and pepper to your taste preferences for a delightful culinary experience.
8. Carefully position the pizza on the hot pizza stone or baking sheet in the oven, using the parchment paper as a foundation, ensuring gentle handling.
9. Place the pizza in the oven and bake for around 12 to 15 minutes, or until the crust turns a delightful golden brown and the cheese is melted and bubbling irresistibly.
10. Remove from the oven and let the pizza cool for a few minutes.
11. Slice the pizza into desired portions and serve hot.

Nutritional breakdown per serving:

Calories: 380 kcal, Protein: 16 grams, Carbohydrates: 41 grams, Fat: 17 grams, Saturated Fat: 6 grams, Cholesterol: 190 milligrams, Sodium: 780 milligrams, Fiber: 3 grams, and Sugar: 2 grams.

PISTACHIO AND POMEGRANATE PIZZA

- Prep Time: 20 minutes
- Cooking Time: 15 minutes
- Total Time: 35 minutes
- Servings: 4

Ingredients:

- 1 prepared pizza dough
- 1/2 cup ricotta cheese
- 1/2 cup shredded mozzarella cheese
- 1/4 cup shelled pistachios, roughly chopped
- 1/4 cup pomegranate arils
- 2 tablespoons honey
- Fresh basil leaves, for garnish
- Salt and pepper to taste

Directions:

1. To ensure optimal results, it is important to preheat the oven to a temperature of 450°F (230°C) before beginning. Position a pizza stone or baking sheet inside the oven and allow it to heat up thoroughly.
2. Gently flatten the pizza dough that has been prepared onto a surface dusted with flour until it reaches your desired thickness. Subsequently, carefully move the dough onto a sheet of parchment paper.
3. In a compact bowl, blend the ricotta cheese with salt and pepper to suit your taste. Carefully distribute the ricotta mixture across the pizza dough, ensuring to maintain a narrow border along the edges.
4. Sprinkle the shredded mozzarella cheese over the ricotta.
5. Sprinkle the chopped pistachios and pomegranate arils on top of the cheese.
6. Drizzle the honey over the pizza.
7. Carefully position the pizza on the hot pizza stone or baking sheet in the oven, using the parchment paper as a foundation, ensuring gentle handling.
8. To cook the pizza, put it in the oven and bake it for approximately 12 to 15 minutes, or until the crust develops a delightful golden brown color and the cheese melts and bubbles irresistibly.
9. Remove from the oven and let the pizza cool for a few minutes.
10. Garnish with fresh basil leaves.
11. Slice the pizza into desired portions and serve hot.

Nutritional breakdown per serving:

Calories: 340 kcal, Protein: 14 grams, Carbohydrates: 38 grams, Fat: 16 grams, Saturated Fat: 6 grams, Cholesterol: 25 milligrams, Sodium: 420 milligrams, Fiber: 2 grams, and Sugar: 13 grams.

MOROCCAN SPICED LAMB PIZZA

- Prep Time: 20 minutes
- Cook Time: 15 minutes
- Total Time: 35 minutes
- Servings: 4

Ingredients:

- 1 pound ground lamb
- 1 tablespoon olive oil
- 1 small onion, finely chopped
- 2 cloves garlic, minced
- 1 teaspoon ground cumin
- 1 teaspoon ground coriander
- 1/2 teaspoon ground cinnamon
- 1/2 teaspoon paprika
- Salt and pepper to taste
- 4 naan bread or pizza crusts
- 1/2 cup tomato sauce
- 1 cup shredded mozzarella cheese
- 1/2 cup crumbled feta cheese
- 1/4 cup sliced black olives
- Fresh cilantro leaves, for garnish

Directions:

1. Make sure to adjust the oven temperature to 425°F (220°C) before you begin cooking.
2. Begin by warming the olive oil in a roomy skillet over medium heat. Next, sauté the finely chopped onion and minced garlic until the onion becomes translucent.
3. Add the ground lamb to the skillet and cook until browned, breaking it up with a spatula. Drain any excess fat.
4. Mix in the ground cumin, ground coriander, ground cinnamon, paprika, salt, and pepper. Continue cooking the meat for an extra 2-3 minutes to let the flavors of the spices infuse and combine.
5. Arrange the naan bread or pizza crusts on a baking sheet, followed by an even and thin layer of tomato sauce spread across each crust.
6. Divide the spiced lamb mixture among the crusts, spreading it out evenly.

7. Sprinkle the shredded mozzarella cheese, crumbled feta cheese, and sliced black olives over the lamb.
8. Put the pizza in the oven and bake for around 12 to 15 minutes, or until the crust turns a delightful golden brown and the cheese bubbles and melts to perfection.
9. Remove from the oven and let the pizzas cool slightly. Garnish with fresh cilantro leaves.
10. Cut into slices and serve hot.

Nutritional breakdown per serving:

Calories: 490 kcal, Protein: 28 grams, Carbohydrates: 41 grams, Fat: 24 grams, Saturated Fat: 10 grams, Cholesterol: 95 milligrams, Sodium: 810 milligrams, Fiber: 33 grams, and Sugar: 4 grams.

SMOKED SALMON AND DILL PIZZA

- Prep Time: 15 minutes
- Cook Time: 12 minutes
- Total Time: 27 minutes
- Servings: 4

Ingredients:

- 1 pre-made pizza crust
- 1/2 cup cream cheese
- 1 tablespoon fresh lemon juice
- 1 teaspoon lemon zest
- 1 tablespoon fresh dill, chopped
- 4 ounces smoked salmon, thinly sliced
- 1/4 red onion, thinly sliced
- 2 tablespoons capers
- Freshly ground black pepper, to taste
- Fresh dill sprigs, for garnish

Directions:

1. Prior to commencing the cooking process, it is important to ensure that the oven temperature is set to 425°F (220°C).
2. Place the pre-made pizza crust on a baking sheet.
3. Take a small bowl and mix the cream cheese, fresh lemon juice, lemon zest, and chopped dill until they are completely blended together.
4. Evenly distribute the cream cheese mixture over the pizza crust.
5. Arrange the smoked salmon slices on top of the cream cheese mixture.
6. Scatter the thinly sliced red onion and capers over the smoked salmon.
7. Season with freshly ground black pepper to taste.
8. Place the pizza in the preheated oven and bake for 12 minutes, or until the crust is golden and crisp.
9. Remove from the oven and let the pizza cool slightly.
10. Garnish with fresh dill sprigs.
11. Slice into pieces and serve warm.

Nutritional breakdown per serving:

Calories: 280 kcal, Protein: 11 grams, Carbohydrates: 29 grams, Fat: 13 grams, Saturated Fat: 6 grams, Cholesterol: 30 milligrams, Sodium: 760 milligrams, Fiber: 1 grams, and Sugar: 3 grams.

ROASTED BEET AND GOAT CHEESE PIZZA

- Prep Time: 15 minutes
- Cook Time: 40 minutes
- Total Time: 55 minutes
- Servings: 4

Ingredients:

- 2 medium beets, roasted and thinly sliced
- 1 pre-made pizza crust
- 4 ounces goat cheese, crumbled
- 1/4 cup chopped walnuts
- 2 cups arugula
- 1 tablespoon balsamic glaze
- Salt and pepper to taste
- Olive oil, for drizzling

Directions:

1. It is essential to set the oven temperature to 425°F (220°C) before you start cooking.
2. Cover the beets with aluminum foil and place them in the preheated oven for approximately 40 minutes, or until they become tender. Allow them to cool, then remove the peel and slice them thinly.
3. Place the pre-made pizza crust on a baking sheet.
4. Spread the crumbled goat cheese evenly over the pizza crust.
5. Arrange the roasted beet slices on top of the goat cheese.
6. Sprinkle the chopped walnuts over the beets.
7. To enhance flavor, adjust salt and pepper to your taste preferences for a delightful culinary experience.
8. Exercise caution while you gradually drizzle a small quantity of olive oil onto the pizza.
9. Place the pizza in the oven and cook it for approximately 12 to 15 minutes, or until the crust achieves a beautiful golden brown color and the cheese becomes bubbly and melted to perfection.
10. Remove from the oven and let the pizza cool slightly.
11. Finish off the dish by adding a generous amount of fresh arugula on top and giving it a delightful drizzle of balsamic glaze.
12. Slice into pieces and serve warm.

Nutritional breakdown per serving:

Calories: 320 kcal, Protein: 12 grams, Carbohydrates: 31 grams, Fat: 17 grams, Saturated Fat: 6 grams, Cholesterol: 31 milligrams, Sodium: 380 milligrams, Fiber: 4 grams, and Sugar: 8 grams.

LEBANESE ZA'ATAR PIZZA

- Prep Time: 15 minutes
- Cook Time: 12 minutes
- Total Time: 27 minutes
- Servings: 4

Ingredients:

- 1 pre-made pizza crust
- 2 tablespoons olive oil
- 2 tablespoons za'atar spice blend
- 1 cup shredded mozzarella cheese
- 1/4 cup crumbled feta cheese
- 1/4 cup sliced black olives
- 1/4 cup chopped fresh parsley
- Lemon wedges, for serving

Directions:

1. Before you start cooking, be sure to set the oven temperature to 425°F (220°C).
2. Place the pre-made pizza crust on a baking sheet.
3. Take a small bowl and combine the olive oil with the za'atar spice mixture, stirring until they are completely mixed together.
4. Brush the za'atar mixture evenly over the pizza crust.
5. Evenly distribute the shredded mozzarella cheese on top of the za'atar mixture.
6. Scatter the crumbled feta cheese and sliced black olives over the mozzarella.
7. Once the pizza is ready, carefully transfer it into the preheated oven and allow it to bake for around 12 minutes. Keep an eye on it and remove it when the crust has achieved a beautiful golden brown color and the cheese has melted, creating a delightful bubbly texture.
8. Remove from the oven and let the pizza cool slightly.
9. Sprinkle the chopped fresh parsley over the pizza.
10. Slice into pieces and serve warm with lemon wedges on the side.

Nutritional breakdown per serving:

Calories: 280 kcal, Protein: 10 grams, Carbohydrates: 29 grams, Fat: 14 grams, Saturated Fat: 5 grams, Cholesterol: 20 milligrams, Sodium: 480 milligrams, Fiber: 2 grams, and Sugar: 1 grams.

GREEK GYRO PIZZA

- Prep Time: 20 minutes
- Cook Time: 15 minutes
- Total Time: 35 minutes
- Servings: 4

Ingredients:

- 1 pre-made pizza dough
- 1/2 cup tzatziki sauce
- 8 ounces cooked gyro meat, thinly sliced
- 1 cup crumbled feta cheese
- 1/2 cup sliced red onions
- 1/2 cup sliced tomatoes
- 1/4 cup sliced Kalamata olives
- 2 tablespoons chopped fresh dill
- Salt and pepper to taste
- Olive oil, for drizzling

Directions:

1. Preheat the oven according to the pre-made pizza dough package instructions.
2. Take a rolling pin and gently roll it over the dough on a floured surface until it is flattened to your preferred thickness.
3. Transfer the rolled-out dough onto a baking sheet or pizza stone.
4. Spread the tzatziki sauce evenly over the pizza dough.
5. Arrange the sliced gyro meat on top of the sauce.
6. Sprinkle the crumbled feta cheese over the gyro meat.
7. Scatter the sliced red onions, tomatoes, and Kalamata olives on the pizza.
8. To enhance flavor, adjust salt and pepper to your taste preferences for a delightful culinary experience.
9. Drizzle a little olive oil over the pizza.
10. Put the pizza in the oven and bake for around 12 to 15 minutes, or until the crust turns a delightful golden brown and the cheese bubbles and melts to perfection.
11. Remove from the oven and let the pizza cool slightly.
12. Sprinkle the chopped fresh dill over the pizza.
13. Slice into pieces and serve warm.

Nutritional breakdown per serving:

Calories: 520 kcal, Protein: 25 grams, Carbohydrates: 40 grams, Fat: 28 grams, Saturated Fat: 12 grams, Cholesterol: 75 milligrams, Sodium: 1260 milligrams, Fiber: 2 grams, and Sugar: 25 grams.

SMOKY EGGPLANT AND HALLOUMI PIZZA

- Prep Time: 20 minutes
- Cook Time: 15 minutes
- Total Time: 35 minutes
- Servings: 4

Ingredients:

- 1 pre-made pizza dough
- 1 medium eggplant, sliced into rounds
- 8 ounces halloumi cheese, sliced
- 1/2 cup tomato sauce
- 2 cloves garlic, minced
- 1 teaspoon smoked paprika
- 1/2 teaspoon dried oregano
- 1/4 teaspoon red pepper flakes (optional)
- Salt and pepper to taste
- Olive oil, for drizzling
- Fresh basil leaves, for garnish

Directions:

1. Preheat the oven according to the pre-made pizza dough package instructions.
2. Place the eggplant rounds on a baking sheet and drizzle with olive oil. Season with salt and pepper.
3. Place the eggplant in the oven that has been preheated and roast it for about 10-12 minutes, or until it becomes tender and develops a light brown color.
4. In a small bowl, mix together the tomato sauce, minced garlic, smoked paprika, dried oregano, and red pepper flakes (if using).
5. Using a rolling pin, flatten the pizza dough on a surface covered with flour until it reaches the thickness you desire.
6. Transfer the rolled-out dough onto a baking sheet or pizza stone.
7. Spread the tomato sauce mixture evenly over the pizza dough.
8. Arrange the roasted eggplant rounds and halloumi cheese slices on top of the sauce.
9. Drizzle a little olive oil over the pizza.
10. Place the pizza in the oven and cook it for approximately 12 to 15 minutes, or until the crust achieves a beautiful golden brown color and the cheese becomes bubbly and melted to perfection.
11. Remove from the oven and let the pizza cool slightly.

12. Garnish with fresh basil leaves.
13. Slice into pieces and serve warm.

Nutritional breakdown per serving:

Calories: 380 kcal, Protein: 18 grams, Carbohydrates: 42 grams, Fat: 16 grams, Saturated Fat: 8 grams, Cholesterol: 40 milligrams, Sodium: 900 milligrams, Fiber: 4 grams, and Sugar: 5 grams.

ROASTED GARLIC AND MUSHROOM PIZZA

- Prep Time: 15 minutes
- Cook Time: 25 minutes
- Total Time: 40 minutes
- Servings: 4

Ingredients:

- 1 pre-made pizza dough
- 8 ounces cremini mushrooms, sliced
- 4 cloves garlic, roasted and minced
- 1 cup shredded mozzarella cheese
- 1/2 cup grated Parmesan cheese
- 2 tablespoons olive oil
- 1 teaspoon dried thyme
- Salt and pepper to taste
- Fresh basil leaves, for garnish

Directions:

1. Preheat the oven according to the pre-made pizza dough package instructions.
2. Flatten the pizza dough on a surface dusted with flour to achieve the thickness you prefer.
3. Transfer the rolled-out dough onto a baking sheet or pizza stone.
4. Heat olive oil in a skillet, sauté mushrooms until golden brown and tender, about 5-7 minutes. Season with salt, pepper, and dried thyme.
5. Spread the minced roasted garlic evenly over the pizza dough.
6. Evenly distribute the shredded mozzarella cheese on top of the garlic.
7. Arrange the sautéed mushrooms on top of the cheese.
8. Sprinkle the grated Parmesan cheese over the mushrooms.
9. Drizzle a little olive oil over the pizza.
10. Oven-bake the dish for 20-25 minutes until the crust turns golden and crispy.
11. Remove from the oven and let the pizza cool slightly.
12. Garnish with fresh basil leaves.
13. Slice into pieces and serve warm.

Nutritional breakdown per serving:

Calories: 320 kcal, Protein: 15 grams, Carbohydrates: 32 grams, Fat: 15 grams, Saturated Fat: 6 grams, Cholesterol: 25 milligrams, Sodium: 570 milligrams, Fiber: 2 grams, and Sugar: 2 grams.

CHAPTER 5:
PASTA BASICS
AND CLASSIC

AGLIO E OLIO

- Prep Time: 5 minutes
- Cook Time: 10 minutes
- Total Time: 15 minutes
- Servings: 4

Ingredients:

- 1 pound spaghetti
- 1/2 cup extra virgin olive oil
- 6 cloves garlic 1, thinly sliced
- 1 teaspoon red pepper flakes
- 1/2 cup chopped fresh parsley
- Salt, to taste
- Grated Parmesan cheese, for serving (optional)

Directions:

1. Begin by bringing a generously salted pot of water to a vigorous boil. Follow the instructions on the spaghetti package to cook it until it reaches the desired al dente consistency. Once cooked, drain the spaghetti and set it aside for later use.
2. Begin by heating olive oil in a large skillet over medium heat. Add garlic slices and red pepper flakes to the skillet. Cook the garlic over medium heat for 2-3 minutes, stirring occasionally, until it becomes golden brown and fragrant. Be mindful not to burn the garlic during the cooking process.
3. After the spaghetti has finished cooking, transfer it to the skillet that already contains the garlic and oil. Mix thoroughly to ensure that the pasta is evenly coated with the oil and garlic.
4. Stir in the chopped parsley and season with salt to taste. Toss again to combine all the ingredients.
5. Remove from heat and transfer the Aglio e Olio to serving plates.
6. Serve hot, garnished with grated Parmesan cheese if desired.

Nutritional breakdown per serving:

Calories: 450 kcal, Protein: 8 grams, Carbohydrates: 60 grams, Fat: 20 grams, Saturated Fat: 3 grams, Cholesterol: 0 milligrams, Sodium: 10 milligrams, Fiber: 3 grams, and Sugar: 2 grams.

SPAGHETTI CARBONARA

- Prep Time: 10 minutes
- Cook Time: 15 minutes
- Total Time: 25 minutes
- Servings: 4

Ingredients:

- 12 ounces spaghetti
- 6 slices bacon, chopped
- 3 cloves garlic, minced
- 3 large eggs
- 1 cup grated Parmesan cheese
- 1/4 cup chopped fresh parsley
- Salt and black pepper, to taste

Directions:

1. To begin, heat a sizable pot of water with salt until it reaches a rolling boil. Proceed to cook the spaghetti until it reaches the desired al dente texture, following the instructions provided on the packaging. Afterward, drain the cooked spaghetti and set it aside for later use.
2. To start, cook the chopped bacon in a large skillet over medium heat until it becomes crispy. After cooking, take out the bacon from the skillet and transfer it onto a plate that has been lined with paper towels. This will help to drain off any extra grease.
3. Using the same skillet, add the minced garlic and cook it for approximately 1 minute until it becomes aromatic.
4. In a bowl of medium size, blend together the eggs, grated Parmesan cheese, and finely chopped parsley. Enhance the flavor by seasoning with a pinch of salt and black pepper.
5. Gently incorporate the cooked spaghetti into the skillet where the garlic resides, making sure to blend it thoroughly to achieve an even coating of the delectable bacon drippings.
6. Remove the skillet from heat and quickly pour the egg mixture over the spaghetti. Toss well to evenly coat the pasta with the egg mixture. As the pasta absorbs the heat, it will gently cook the eggs, resulting in a luscious and creamy sauce.
7. Add the crispy bacon back to the skillet and toss to combine.
8. Present the Spaghetti Carbonara promptly, adorned with extra grated Parmesan cheese and finely chopped parsley, if preferred.

Nutritional breakdown per serving:

Calories: 550 kcal, Protein: 28 grams, Carbohydrates: 57 grams, Fat: 23 grams, Saturated Fat: 9 grams, Cholesterol: 180 milligrams, Sodium: 700 milligrams, Fiber: 3 grams, and Sugar: 2 grams.

LINGUINE ALLE VONGOLE

- Prep Time: 15 minutes
- Cook Time: 15 minutes
- Total Time: 30 minutes
- Servings: 4

Ingredients:

- 12 ounces linguine
- 2 pounds fresh clams, scrubbed and rinsed
- 4 tablespoons extra virgin olive oil
- 4 cloves garlic, minced
- 1/2 teaspoon red pepper flakes
- 1/2 cup dry white wine
- 1/4 cup chopped fresh parsley
- Salt, to taste

Directions:

1. To start, bring a generous pot of water seasoned with salt to a boiling point. Proceed to cook the linguine according to the instructions on the package until it reaches the perfect al dente texture. Once cooked, drain the linguine and set it aside for later use.
2. To begin, warm the olive oil in a spacious skillet over medium heat. Introduce the minced garlic and red pepper flakes, allowing them to cook for approximately one minute until the garlic emits a delightful aroma.
3. Add the clams to the skillet and pour in the white wine. Cover the skillet and cook for about 5-7 minutes, or until the clams open. Discard any clams that do not open.
4. Remove the cooked clams from the skillet and set aside. Keep the skillet with the clam cooking liquid on the heat.
5. Add the cooked linguine to the skillet with the clam cooking liquid. Toss well to coat the pasta with the flavors from the clams.
6. Stir in the chopped parsley and season with salt to taste. Toss again to combine all the ingredients.
7. Remove from heat and transfer the Linguine alle Vongole to serving plates.
8. Serve hot, garnished with additional chopped parsley if desired.

Nutritional breakdown per serving:

Calories: 450 kcal, Protein: 20 grams, Carbohydrates: 60 grams, Fat: 12 grams, Saturated Fat: 2 grams, Cholesterol: 40 milligrams, Sodium: 300 milligrams, Fiber: 2 grams, and Sugar: 1 grams.

PASTA PUTTANESCA

- Prep Time: 10 minutes
- Cook Time: 15 minutes
- Total Time: 25 minutes
- Servings: 4

Ingredients:

- 12 ounces spaghetti or linguine
- 2 tablespoons extra virgin olive oil
- 4 cloves garlic, minced
- 1/2 teaspoon red pepper flakes
- 1 can (14 ounces) diced tomatoes
- 1/2 cup pitted Kalamata olives, halved
- 2 tablespoons capers, drained
- 2 tablespoons chopped fresh parsley
- Salt, to taste
- Grated Parmesan cheese, for serving (optional)

Directions:

1. To get started, fill a pot with water and bring it to a boil. Add salt to the boiling water based on your preference. Observe the directions given on the pasta package to achieve the perfect al dente texture. Drain and set aside after cooking.
2. Gather the basil leaves, grated Parmesan cheese, pine nuts, and garlic, and place them in a food processor or blender. Process the mixture until the ingredients are finely chopped and fully integrated, resulting in a delightful combination of flavors and textures that come together harmoniously.
3. While the food processor or blender is running, gradually pour in olive oil until the mixture achieves a smooth consistency. Enhance the flavor of the mixture by adding salt and pepper to suit your personal taste. This will elevate the taste profile, making it more enjoyable.
4. In a spacious mixing bowl, blend the cooked pasta with the pesto sauce. Toss thoroughly to ensure the pasta is evenly coated with the sauce.
5. To incorporate the cooked pasta into the skillet, make sure it is evenly coated with the puttanesca sauce by tossing it well.
6. Remove from heat and sprinkle with chopped parsley.
7. Serve hot, garnished with grated Parmesan cheese if desired.

Nutritional breakdown per serving:

Calories: 350 kcal, Protein: 10 grams, Carbohydrates: 55 grams, Fat: 10 grams, Saturated Fat: 1.5 grams, Cholesterol: 0 milligrams, Sodium: 800 milligrams, Fiber: 5 grams, and Sugar: 4 grams.

PESTO PASTA

- Prep Time: 10 minutes
- Cook Time: 10 minutes
- Total Time: 20 minutes
- Servings: 4

Ingredients:

- 12 ounces pasta (such as spaghetti or penne)
- 2 cups fresh basil leaves
- 1/2 cup grated Parmesan cheese
- 1/4 cup pine nuts
- 2 cloves garlic
- 1/2 cup extra virgin olive oil
- Salt and pepper, to taste
- Optional toppings: cherry tomatoes, sliced black olives, grated Parmesan cheese

Directions:

1. To begin, fill a large pot with water and bring it to a boil. Add salt to the water and follow the pasta package instructions for cooking time. After cooking the pasta, remove the water by draining it and then set the pasta aside for later use.
2. Gather the basil leaves, grated Parmesan cheese, pine nuts, and garlic, and place them in a food processor or blender. Process the mixture until the ingredients are finely chopped and fully integrated, resulting in a delightful combination of flavors and textures that come together harmoniously.
3. While the food processor or blender is running, gradually pour in olive oil until the mixture achieves a smooth consistency. Enhance the flavor of the mixture by adding salt and pepper to suit your personal taste. This will elevate the taste profile, making it more enjoyable.
4. In a spacious mixing bowl, blend the cooked pasta with the pesto sauce. Toss thoroughly to ensure the pasta is evenly coated with the sauce.
5. Optional: Add cherry tomatoes, sliced black olives, or grated Parmesan cheese as desired for additional flavor and texture.
6. Serve the pesto pasta immediately while it is still warm.

Nutritional breakdown per serving:

Calories: 450 kcal, Protein: 10 grams, Carbohydrates: 40 grams, Fat: 30 grams, Saturated Fat: 5 grams, Cholesterol: 10 milligrams, Sodium: 200 milligrams, Fiber: 3 grams, and Sugar: 2 grams.

FETTUCCINE ALFREDO

- Prep Time: 10 minutes
- Cook Time: 15 minutes
- Total Time: 25 minutes
- Servings: 4

Ingredients:

- 12 ounces fettuccine pasta
- 1/2 cup unsalted butter
- 1 cup heavy cream
- 1 cup grated Parmesan cheese
- Salt and pepper, to taste
- Chopped fresh parsley, for garnish (optional)

Directions:

1. Start by filling a pot with salted water and bringing it to a rolling boil. Prepare the fettuccine pasta by following the instructions on the package for cooking it until it reaches the desired al dente texture. After the pasta is cooked, carefully drain the water and reserve it for later. Set the pasta aside, ready to be used when needed.
2. To start, heat the butter in a spacious skillet over medium heat until it melts completely. Following that, introduce the heavy cream to the skillet and let it gently simmer.
3. Lower the heat and whisk in the grated Parmesan cheese until fully melted, resulting in a flavorful and smooth sauce. To achieve the ideal flavor, sprinkle salt and pepper according to your personal preference. This will ensure a well-seasoned dish that suits your taste buds.
4. After cooking the fettuccine pasta, combine it with the Alfredo sauce in the skillet. Mix thoroughly to ensure that the pasta is evenly coated with the sauce.
5. Cook for an additional 2-3 minutes, stirring gently, until the pasta is heated through.
6. Take the dish off the heat and, if desired, add a finishing touch by sprinkling it with freshly chopped parsley.
7. Serve the Fettuccine Alfredo immediately while it is still warm.

Nutritional breakdown per serving:

Calories: 650 kcal, Protein: 17 grams, Carbohydrates: 44 grams, Fat: 47 grams, Saturated Fat: 29 grams, Cholesterol: 155 milligrams, Sodium: 550 milligrams, Fiber: 2 grams, and Sugar: 2 grams.

PASTA PRIMAVERA

- Prep Time: 15 minutes
- Cook Time: 15 minutes
- Total Time: 30 minutes
- Servings: 4

Ingredients:

- 8 ounces pasta (such as penne or fettuccine)
- 2 tablespoons olive oil
- 2 cloves garlic, minced
- 1 small onion, thinly sliced
- 1 cup sliced bell peppers (assorted colors)
- 1 cup sliced zucchini
- 1 cup sliced mushrooms
- 1 cup cherry tomatoes, halved
- 1/2 cup vegetable broth
- 1/4 cup grated Parmesan cheese
- 1/4 cup chopped fresh basil
- Salt and pepper, to taste

Directions:

1. To prepare the pasta, fill a pot with water and add salt. Heat the water until it reaches boiling point. Refer to the instructions on the packaging for the recommended cooking time to achieve the desired level of doneness, commonly known as "al dente." Once the pasta is cooked, drain the water and set the pasta aside for future use.
2. In a spacious skillet, warm the olive oil over medium heat. Introduce the minced garlic and sliced onion to the skillet. Sauté the mixture for approximately 2-3 minutes, or until the onion turns translucent.
3. Add the sliced bell peppers, zucchini, and mushrooms to the skillet. Cook for 5-6 minutes until the vegetables are tender-crisp.
4. Add the cherry tomatoes and vegetable broth to the skillet. Cook for an additional 2-3 minutes until the tomatoes are slightly softened.
5. To bring everything together, incorporate the cooked pasta with the sautéed vegetables in the skillet. Ensure that the mixture is thoroughly mixed to achieve an even distribution.
6. Stir in the grated Parmesan cheese and chopped fresh basil. Season with salt and pepper to taste.

7. Continue cooking for an additional 1-2 minutes, or until the cheese has melted and the pasta is thoroughly heated.
8. Serve the Pasta Primavera immediately while it is still warm.

Nutritional breakdown per serving:

Calories: 350 kcal, Protein: 12 grams, Carbohydrates: 55 grams, Fat: 10 grams, Saturated Fat: 2 grams, Cholesterol: 5 milligrams, Sodium: 200 milligrams, Fiber: 5 grams, and Sugar: 6 grams.

BUCATINI ALL'AMATRICIANA

- Prep Time: 10 minutes
- Cook Time: 25 minutes
- Total Time: 35 minutes
- Servings: 4

Ingredients:

- 12 ounces bucatini pasta
- 4 ounces pancetta or guanciale, diced
- 1 small onion, finely chopped
- 2 cloves garlic, minced
- 1/2 teaspoon red pepper flakes
- 1 can (14 ounces) crushed tomatoes
- 1/4 cup grated Pecorino Romano cheese
- Salt and pepper, to taste
- Fresh parsley, chopped (for garnish)

Directions:

1. To begin, fill a sizable pot with water and add a pinch of salt. Heat the water until it reaches a boiling point. To achieve the desired texture, follow the pasta package instructions and cook until al dente. Once cooked, carefully drain the pasta and then set it aside for future use.
2. In a spacious skillet, cook the diced pancetta or guanciale over medium heat until it becomes crispy. After achieving the desired crispness of the pancetta, set it aside while keeping the rendered fat in the skillet.
3. In the skillet, add the chopped onion and minced garlic. Continue cooking until the onion becomes translucent and the garlic releases its aromatic fragrance.
4. Add the red pepper flakes to the skillet and cook for an additional minute.
5. Pour in the crushed tomatoes and bring the sauce to a simmer. Cook for about 10 minutes, stirring occasionally.
6. Reincorporate the cooked pancetta into the skillet and stir it together with the sauce.
7. Customize the flavor of the sauce by adding salt and pepper to your liking.
8. Add the cooked bucatini pasta to the skillet with the sauce. Thoroughly mix the pasta and sauce together to ensure the pasta is evenly coated.
9. Present the Bucatini all'Amatriciana while still hot, adorned with grated Pecorino Romano cheese and freshly chopped parsley as a garnish.

Nutritional breakdown per serving:

Calories: 450 kcal, Protein: 15 grams, Carbohydrates: 70 grams, Fat: 12 grams, Saturated Fat: 4 grams, Cholesterol: 20 milligrams, Sodium: 600 milligrams, Fiber: 4 grams, and Sugar: 6 grams.

LASAGNA

- Prep Time: 30 minutes
- Cook Time: 1 hour
- Total Time: 1 hour 30 minutes
- Servings: 8

Ingredients:

- 12 lasagna noodles
- 1 pound ground beef
- 1 onion, chopped
- 3 cloves garlic, minced
- 1 can (28 ounces) crushed tomatoes
- 1 can (6 ounces) tomato paste
- 1/2 cup water
- 2 teaspoons dried basil
- 2 teaspoons dried oregano
- 1 teaspoon salt
- 1/2 teaspoon black pepper
- 2 cups ricotta cheese
- 2 cups shredded mozzarella cheese
- 1/2 cup grated Parmesan cheese
- Fresh parsley, chopped

Directions:

1. To ensure proper cooking, it is recommended to set the oven temperature to 375°F (190°C) ahead of time.
2. To achieve the desired texture, cook the lasagna noodles following the instructions on the package until they are al dente. After cooking, remove the excess water from the noodles by draining them, and then keep them aside for future use.
3. In a spacious frying pan, cook the ground beef on medium heat until it turns brown. Add the chopped onion and minced garlic. Cook until the onion becomes translucent.
4. Add crushed tomatoes, tomato paste, water, dried basil, dried oregano, salt, and black pepper. For a perfect fusion of flavors, gently simmer the sauce for 15 to 20 minutes, making sure to stir it occasionally throughout the cooking process.
5. In a separate bowl, mix the ricotta cheese, 1 1/2 cups of shredded mozzarella cheese, and 1/4 cup of grated Parmesan cheese until they are thoroughly incorporated.

6. Ensure the bottom of a 9x13-inch baking dish is evenly covered with a thin layer of the meat sauce. Place 4 lasagna noodles on the sauce in a neat arrangement.
7. Spread half of the cheese mixture over the noodles. Top with a third of the remaining meat sauce.
8. Repeat the layers with 4 more lasagna noodles, the remaining cheese mixture, and another third of the meat sauce.
9. Place the remaining 4 lasagna noodles on top, then generously spread the remaining meat sauce over them. Sprinkle the remaining shredded mozzarella and grated Parmesan cheese evenly on top, covering the entire area.
10. Bake the dish covered for 25 minutes, then uncover and bake for an extra 10-15 minutes until the cheese is melted and bubbly.
11. Let the lasagna rest for 10 minutes before serving. Garnish with fresh parsley.

Nutritional breakdown per serving:

Calories: 450 kcal, Protein: 30 grams, Carbohydrates: 38 grams, Fat: 20 grams, Saturated Fat: 10 grams, Cholesterol: 80 milligrams, Sodium: 900 milligrams, Fiber: 4 grams, and Sugar: 8 grams.

RAVIOLI WITH SAGE BUTTER SAUCE

- Prep Time: 15 minutes
- Cook Time: 10 minutes
- Total Time: 25 minutes
- Servings: 4

Ingredients:

- 1 package (16 ounces) fresh or frozen ravioli (your choice of filling)
- 4 tablespoons unsalted butter
- 8-10 fresh sage leaves
- 1/4 cup grated Parmesan cheese
- Salt and pepper, to taste

Directions:

1. To begin, fill a large pot with water and bring it to a boil. Add salt to the water and follow the pasta package instructions for cooking time. After cooking the pasta, remove the water by draining it and then set the pasta aside for later use.
2. In a big skillet, melt the butter on medium heat. Cook the sage leaves until the butter turns golden brown and the leaves become crispy. Be careful not to burn the butter.
3. Remove the skillet from heat and carefully remove the sage leaves from the butter. Set the sage leaves aside for garnish.
4. Place the skillet back on low heat and add the cooked ravioli to the butter sauce. Gently toss the ravioli in the sauce until they are evenly coated.
5. Customize the flavor by adding salt and pepper to suit your personal preferences.
6. Serve the ravioli hot, garnished with the crispy sage leaves and grated Parmesan cheese.

Nutritional breakdown per serving:

Calories: 400 kcal, Protein: 15 grams, Carbohydrates: 40 grams, Fat: 20 grams, Saturated Fat: 12 grams, Cholesterol: 80 milligrams, Sodium: 500 milligrams, Fiber: 2 grams, and Sugar: 2 grams.

CHAPTER 6: MEDITERRANEAN PASTA SAUCES

MARINARA SAUCE

- Prep Time: 10 minutes
- Cook Time: 30 minutes
- Total Time: 40 minutes
- Servings: 6

Ingredients:

- 2 tablespoons olive oil
- 1 small onion, finely chopped
- 3 cloves garlic, minced
- 1 can (28 ounces) crushed tomatoes
- 1 can (14 ounces) diced tomatoes
- 2 tablespoons tomato paste
- 1 teaspoon dried basil
- 1 teaspoon dried oregano
- 1/2 teaspoon sugar
- Salt and pepper, to taste
- Fresh basil leaves, chopped (for garnish)

Directions:

1. To begin, heat olive oil in a large saucepan over medium heat. Add the diced onion and minced garlic. Continue cooking until the onion turns translucent and the garlic emits its delightful aroma.
2. Add the crushed tomatoes, diced tomatoes, and tomato paste to the saucepan. Stir well to combine.
3. Add the dried basil, dried oregano, sugar, salt, and pepper to the sauce. Stir to incorporate the seasonings.
4. Once the sauce reaches a simmer, lower the heat to a gentle simmer. Ensure the saucepan is covered and let it simmer for around 20-30 minutes, remembering to stir occasionally.
5. Give the sauce a taste and make any necessary adjustments to the seasonings.
6. Remove the sauce from the heat and let it cool for a short duration. If you so choose, you have the option to utilize either an immersion blender or a conventional blender to blend the sauce until it achieves a smooth and uniform texture.
7. Serve the marinara sauce hot over pasta or use it as a base for other dishes. Garnish with fresh chopped basil.

Nutritional breakdown per serving:

Calories: 70 kcal, Protein: 2 grams, Carbohydrates: 8 grams, Fat: 4 grams, Saturated Fat: 0.5 grams, Cholesterol: 20 milligrams, Sodium: 320 milligrams, Fiber: 2 grams, and Sugar: 5 grams.

PESTO SAUCE

- Prep Time: 10 minutes
- Total Time: 10 minutes
- Servings: Makes about 1 cup

Ingredients:

- 2 cups fresh basil leaves, packed
- 1/2 cup grated Parmesan cheese
- 1/2 cup extra-virgin olive oil
- 1/3 cup pine nuts
- 3 cloves garlic, minced
- Salt and pepper, to taste

Directions:

1. Blend the basil leaves, Parmesan cheese, pine nuts, and minced garlic together using a food processor or blender. Process the mixture for a few cycles until the ingredients are coarsely chopped and thoroughly combined.
2. Slowly add olive oil to the running food processor until the mixture becomes smooth and well blended. To ensure that all the ingredients are thoroughly combined, it may be necessary to scrape down the sides of the processor bowl with a spatula.
3. Customize the flavor of the pesto by adding salt and pepper to your preference. Feel at liberty to modify the seasoning to suit your personal taste.
4. Place the pesto into a jar or a container with a secure seal, and keep it refrigerated until you are ready to use it.

Nutritional breakdown per serving:

Calories: 80 kcal, Protein: 2 grams, Carbohydrates: 1 grams, Fat: 8 grams, Saturated Fat: 1.5 grams, Cholesterol: 2 milligrams, Sodium: 70 milligrams, Fiber: 0 grams, and Sugar: 0 grams.

ARRABBIATA SAUCE

- Prep Time: 10 minutes
- Cook Time: 30 minutes
- Total Time: 40 minutes
- Servings: 4

Ingredients:

- 2 tablespoons olive oil
- 4 cloves garlic, minced
- 1/2 teaspoon red pepper flakes
- 1 can (28 ounces) crushed tomatoes
- 1 teaspoon dried basil
- 1 teaspoon dried oregano
- 1/2 teaspoon sugar
- Salt, to taste
- Freshly ground black pepper, to taste
- Fresh basil leaves, chopped (for garnish)
- Grated Parmesan cheese (for serving)

Directions:

1. Start the process by warming up the olive oil in a sizable saucepan over medium heat. Then, introduce the minced garlic and red pepper flakes. Allow them to cook for around 1 minute until the garlic becomes fragrant and releases its enticing aroma.
2. Incorporate the crushed tomatoes into the saucepan and stir thoroughly to ensure proper blending.
3. Add the dried basil, dried oregano, sugar, salt, and black pepper to the sauce. Stir to incorporate the seasonings.
4. Once the sauce reaches a simmer, lower the heat to a gentle simmer. Cover the saucepan and let it simmer for 20-30 minutes, stirring occasionally.
5. Take a small taste of the sauce and make any necessary adjustments to the seasonings.
6. Remove the sauce from the stove or heat source and let it cool for a brief interval.
7. Serve the arrabbiata sauce while it's still hot, generously drizzling it over cooked pasta. Elevate the visual appeal by adorning the dish with delicately minced fresh basil and a light dusting of grated Parmesan cheese.

Nutritional breakdown per serving:

Calories: 100 kcal, Protein: 2 grams, Carbohydrates: 9 grams, Fat: 7 grams, Saturated Fat: 1 grams, Cholesterol: 35 milligrams, Sodium: 480 milligrams, Fiber: 2 grams, and Sugar: 5 grams.

PUTTANESCA SAUCE

- Prep Time: 10 minutes
- Cook Time: 20 minutes
- Total Time: 30 minutes
- Servings: 4

Ingredients:

- 2 tablespoons olive oil
- 4 cloves garlic, minced
- 1/2 teaspoon red pepper flakes
- 6 anchovy fillets, chopped
- 1 can (14 ounces) diced tomatoes
- 1/2 cup pitted Kalamata olives, halved
- 2 tablespoons capers, drained
- 2 tablespoons chopped fresh parsley
- Salt, to taste
- Freshly ground black pepper, to taste
- Grated Parmesan cheese (for serving)

Directions:

1. In a spacious frying pan, warm the olive oil over a medium flame. Introduce the finely chopped garlic and red pepper flakes. Sauté for about 1 minute until the garlic becomes fragrant.
2. Pour the diced tomatoes, along with their juice, into the frying pan. Mix thoroughly to ensure proper integration.
3. Place the diced tomatoes, including their juice, into the skillet. Thoroughly mix to ensure proper incorporation.
4. Heat the sauce until it reaches a simmer, then decrease the heat to a low setting. Let the sauce gently simmer for around 15 minutes, ensuring that you stir it periodically.
5. Add the Kalamata olives, capers, and chopped parsley to the sauce. Stir to incorporate the ingredients.
6. Season the sauce with salt and black pepper to taste. Adjust the seasoning as desired.
7. Maintain the sauce at a simmer for an extra 5 minutes, enabling the flavors to meld together in perfect harmony.
8. Remove the sauce from heat and let it cool slightly.
9. Serve the puttanesca sauce hot over cooked pasta. Top with grated Parmesan cheese.

Nutritional breakdown per serving:

Calories: 180 kcal, Protein: 5 grams, Carbohydrates: 14 grams, Fat: 12 grams, Saturated Fat: 2 grams, Cholesterol: 12 milligrams, Sodium: 900 milligrams, Fiber: 4 grams, and Sugar: 6 grams.

LEMON GARLIC SAUCE

- Prep Time: 5 minutes
- Cook Time: 10 minutes
- Total Time: 15 minutes
- Servings: Makes about 1 cup

Ingredients:

- 4 tablespoons unsalted butter
- 4 cloves garlic, minced
- Zest of 1 lemon
- Juice of 1 lemon
- 1/2 cup chicken or vegetable broth
- Salt, to taste
- Freshly ground black pepper, to taste
- Chopped fresh parsley, for garnish (optional)

Directions:

1. To change the butter into a liquid consistency, gently heat it in a small saucepan over medium heat until it completely melts and becomes a liquid.
2. Incorporate the minced garlic into the melted butter and sauté it for approximately 1 minute, or until it emits a pleasant aroma.
3. Add the lemon zest, lemon juice, and chicken or vegetable broth to the saucepan. Stir well to combine.
4. Simmer the sauce and allow it to cook for approximately 5 minutes, occasionally stirring it.
5. Feel free to enhance the flavor of the sauce by adding salt and black pepper to suit your taste. Adjust the seasoning according to your personal preference to achieve the desired taste.
6. Take the sauce off the heat source and allow it to cool down for a brief amount of time.
7. Serve the lemon garlic sauce warm over grilled chicken, fish, or vegetables. Garnish with chopped fresh parsley, if desired.

Nutritional breakdown per serving:

Calories: 100 kcal, Protein: 1 grams, Carbohydrates: 2 grams, Fat: 10 grams, Saturated Fat: 6 grams, Cholesterol: 15 milligrams, Sodium: 200 milligrams, Fiber: 0 grams, and Sugar: 0 grams.

ALFREDO SAUCE

- Prep Time: 5 minutes
- Cook Time: 10 minutes
- Total Time: 15 minutes
- Servings: Makes about 2 cups

Ingredients:

- 1/2 cup unsalted butter
- 4 cloves garlic, minced
- 2 cups heavy cream
- 1 cup grated Parmesan cheese
- Salt, to taste
- Freshly ground black pepper, to taste
- Chopped fresh parsley, for garnish (optional)

Directions:

1. Apply moderate heat to a saucepan and let the butter melt until it transforms into a liquid state.
2. Sauté the minced garlic in the melted butter for approximately one minute, or until it becomes aromatic.
3. To create a uniform mixture with the garlic and butter, carefully pour the heavy cream into the saucepan and stir it well.
4. Gently simmer the mixture and allow it to cook for around 5 minutes, giving it an occasional stir.
5. Gradually incorporate the grated Parmesan cheese into the mixture, whisking slowly until it fully melts and the sauce achieves a smooth, velvety consistency.
6. Customize the seasoning of the sauce by adding salt and black pepper to match your personal taste, and don't hesitate to make any necessary modifications to achieve the flavor you desire.
7. Remove the sauce from the heat source and let it cool for a short amount of time.
8. Serve the Alfredo sauce warm over cooked pasta. Garnish with chopped fresh parsley, if desired.

Nutritional breakdown per serving:

Calories: 150 kcal, Protein: 3 grams, Carbohydrates: 2 grams, Fat: 15 grams, Saturated Fat: 10 grams, Cholesterol: 25 milligrams, Sodium: 200 milligrams, Fiber: 0 grams, and Sugar: 1 grams.

TOMATO AND BASIL SAUCE

- Prep Time: 10 minutes
- Cook Time: 30 minutes
- Total Time: 40 minutes
- Servings: Makes about 2 cups

Ingredients:

- 2 tablespoons olive oil
- 1 small onion, finely chopped
- 4 cloves garlic, minced
- 1 can (28 ounces) crushed tomatoes
- 1/4 cup tomato paste
- 1/4 cup chopped fresh basil leaves
- 1 teaspoon dried oregano
- Salt, to taste
- Freshly ground black pepper, to taste

Directions:

1. Use medium heat to warm up the olive oil in a large saucepan until it reaches a warm temperature.
2. Place the diced onion in the saucepan and cook it over medium heat for approximately 5 minutes, or until it turns soft and tender.
3. Add the minced garlic to the saucepan and cook for an additional minute, allowing it to release its fragrant aroma.
4. Empty the crushed tomatoes and tomato paste into the saucepan. Mix thoroughly to ensure proper integration.
5. Add the chopped fresh basil leaves and dried oregano to the saucepan. Stir well to incorporate the herbs into the sauce.
6. Personalize the taste of the sauce by incorporating salt and black pepper to match your preferences. Adjust the seasoning as needed to achieve your desired flavor.
7. Let the sauce come to a mild simmer and cook for around 30 minutes, making sure to stir it occasionally.
8. Take the sauce off the stove or burner and allow it to cool for a brief duration.
9. Serve the Tomato and Basil Sauce warm over cooked pasta or use it as a base for other dishes.

Nutritional breakdown per serving (1/4 cup):

Calories: 60 kcal, Protein: 2 grams, Carbohydrates: 8 grams, Fat: 3 grams, Saturated Fat: 0 grams, Cholesterol: 0 milligrams, Sodium: 200 milligrams, Fiber: 2 grams, and Sugar: 4 grams.

GARLIC AND WHITE WINE SAUCE

- Prep Time: 5 minutes
- Cook Time: 15 minutes
- Total Time: 20 minutes
- Servings: Makes about 1 cup

Ingredients:

- 2 tablespoons olive oil
- 4 cloves garlic, minced
- 1/2 cup dry white wine
- 1 cup chicken or vegetable broth
- 2 tablespoons unsalted butter
- 2 tablespoons all-purpose flour
- Salt, to taste
- Freshly ground black pepper, to taste
- Chopped fresh parsley, for garnish (optional)

Directions:

1. Place the saucepan on the stove and apply medium heat to warm the olive oil until it reaches the desired temperature.
2. Incorporate the minced garlic into the saucepan and cook it over medium heat for approximately 1 minute, or until it releases a fragrant aroma.
3. Pour in the white wine and let it simmer for about 2 minutes to reduce slightly.
4. Take a separate small bowl and whisk together the broth, butter, and flour until they are thoroughly combined.
5. Slowly pour the broth mixture into the saucepan while continuously whisking to ensure that no lumps form.
6. To attain the desired consistency for the sauce, it is recommended to let it gently simmer for approximately 10 minutes, ensuring that you stir it intermittently.
7. Tailor the taste of the sauce to your liking by incorporating salt and black pepper. Feel free to adjust the seasoning according to your personal preferences without any hesitation.
8. Remove the sauce from the stove or heat source and let it cool for a short amount of time.
9. Serve the Garlic and White Wine Sauce warm over cooked pasta, chicken, fish, or vegetables. Garnish with chopped fresh parsley, if desired.

Nutritional breakdown per serving (2 tablespoons):

Calories: 70 kcal, Protein: 1 grams, Carbohydrates: 3 grams, Fat: 5 grams, Saturated Fat: 2 grams, Cholesterol: 10 milligrams, Sodium: 150 milligrams, Fiber: 0 grams, and Sugar: 0 grams.

MUSHROOM AND THYME SAUCE

- Prep Time: 10 minutes
- Cook Time: 20 minutes
- Total Time: 30 minutes
- Servings: Makes about 1 cup

Ingredients:

- 2 tablespoons butter
- 8 ounces mushrooms, sliced
- 2 cloves garlic, minced
- 1 teaspoon fresh thyme leaves
- 1 cup vegetable or chicken broth
- 1/2 cup heavy cream
- Salt, to taste
- Freshly ground black pepper, to taste

Directions:

1. Put the butter in a saucepan and apply medium heat, heating it until it fully melts.
2. Add the sliced mushrooms to the saucepan and sauté for about 5 minutes until they start to brown.
3. Incorporate the minced garlic and fresh thyme leaves into the saucepan. Cook for an extra minute, stirring, until a pleasant aroma develops.
4. Pour the vegetable or chicken broth into the pot and bring it to a simmer. Let it simmer for around 10 minutes until the mushrooms are tender and the liquid has slightly reduced.
5. Lower the heat to a low setting and incorporate the heavy cream while stirring. Let the sauce continue simmering for an extra 5 minutes until it achieves a slightly thicker consistency.
6. Customize the flavor of the sauce by adding salt and black pepper to match your individual preferences. Modify the seasoning as needed to achieve the desired taste.
7. Remove the sauce from the stove or heat source and let it cool for a short period of time.
8. Serve the Mushroom and Thyme Sauce warm over cooked pasta, chicken, steak, or vegetables.

Nutritional Value per Serving (2 tablespoons):

Calories: 80 kcal, Protein: 1 grams, Carbohydrates: 3 grams, Fat: 7 grams, Saturated Fat: 4 grams, Cholesterol: 10 milligrams, Sodium: 150 milligrams, Fiber: 0 grams, and Sugar: 1 grams.

ROASTED RED PEPPER SAUCE

- Prep Time: 10 minutes
- Cook Time: 25 minutes
- Total Time: 35 minutes
- Servings: Makes about 1 cup

Ingredients:

- 2 large red bell peppers
- 2 tablespoons olive oil
- 1 small onion, diced
- 2 cloves garlic, minced
- 1/2 teaspoon smoked paprika
- 1/4 teaspoon cayenne pepper (optional, for heat)
- 1/2 cup vegetable broth
- 1 tablespoon tomato paste
- Salt, to taste
- Freshly ground black pepper, to taste

Directions:

1. To initiate the preheating process, modify the oven temperature to 450°F (230°C). Place the red bell peppers onto a baking sheet and cook them for around 20 minutes, ensuring you flip them occasionally, until the skins turn charred and blistered.
2. Remove the roasted red bell peppers from the oven and transfer them to a bowl. Cover the bowl with plastic wrap, enabling the peppers to steam for around 10 minutes. This will make it easier to remove the skins.
3. Once the peppers have cooled slightly, peel off the charred skins and discard them. To prepare the peppers, carefully detach the stems and remove the seeds.
4. Place the saucepan on the stove and heat the olive oil over medium heat. Sauté the diced onion and minced garlic in the saucepan for approximately 5 minutes, until the onion becomes translucent and releases a pleasant aroma.
5. Incorporate the roasted red bell peppers, smoked paprika, and cayenne pepper (if desired) into the saucepan. Mix well to combine.
6. Gently pour the vegetable broth into the mixture and add the tomato paste. Stir thoroughly to ensure all the ingredients are well combined.
7. Let the mixture reach a simmer and continue cooking for around 10 minutes, giving it an occasional stir. This process will allow the flavors to meld together, resulting in a harmonious blend.

8. Take the saucepan off the stove and allow the mixture to cool down for a brief period.
9. Move the mixture into a blender or food processor and continue blending until it reaches a smooth and velvety consistency. Optionally, you can strain the sauce through a fine-mesh sieve to eliminate any remaining solid particles.
10. Incorporate salt and black pepper into the sauce based on your personal taste preferences. Feel free to adjust the seasoning as needed.
11. Serve the Roasted Red Pepper Sauce warm or at room temperature. It can be used as a dip, spread, or sauce for pasta, grilled vegetables, or meats.

Nutritional Value per Serving (2 tablespoons):

Calories: 60 kcal, Protein: 1 grams, Carbohydrates: 6 grams, Fat: 4 grams, Saturated Fat: 1 grams, Cholesterol: 5 milligrams, Sodium: 150 milligrams, Fiber: 1 grams, and Sugar: 3 grams.

CHAPTER 7: PASTA WITH SEAFOOD

LINGUINE WITH SHRIMP SCAMPI

- Prep Time: 15 minutes
- Cook Time: 15 minutes
- Total Time: 30 minutes
- Servings: 4

Ingredients:

- 8 ounces linguine pasta
- 1 pound large shrimp 1, peeled and deveined
- 4 tablespoons unsalted butter
- 4 cloves garlic, minced
- 1/4 teaspoon red pepper flakes
- 1/4 cup fresh lemon juice
- 1/4 cup dry white wine (optional)
- Salt, to taste
- Freshly ground black pepper, to taste
- 2 tablespoons chopped fresh parsley
- Grated Parmesan cheese, for serving

Directions:

1. Prepare the linguine pasta by following the instructions on the package until it reaches the desired al dente texture. After cooking, remove the pasta from the water and separate it by draining. Keep it aside for later use.
2. Place the butter in a large skillet and heat it over medium heat until it completely melts. Next, include the finely chopped garlic and red pepper flakes (if preferred) into the skillet. Sauté the mixture for approximately 1 minute, or until the garlic releases its aromatic fragrance.
3. Place the shrimp in the skillet and cook each side for approximately 2-3 minutes until they transform into a pink and opaque color. Take out the shrimp from the skillet and keep them aside.
4. Pour the lemon juice and white wine (if using) into the skillet. Bring it to a simmer and let it cook for about 2 minutes to reduce slightly.
5. Return the cooked linguine pasta to the skillet and combine it with the sauce to ensure it is evenly coated. Let it cook for an extra 1-2 minutes to make sure the pasta is heated evenly.
6. Season the pasta with salt and black pepper to taste. Adjust the seasoning as desired.
7. Incorporate the cooked shrimp back into the skillet and gently mix it with the pasta.

8. Remove the skillet from heat and sprinkle the chopped fresh parsley over the pasta.
9. Serve the Linguine with Shrimp Scampi hot, garnished with grated Parmesan cheese.

Nutritional Value per Serving:

Calories: 420 kcal, Protein: 26 grams, Carbohydrates: 47 grams, Fat: 14 grams, Saturated Fat: 8 grams, Cholesterol: 220 milligrams, Sodium: 300 milligrams, Fiber: 2 grams, and Sugar: 2 grams.

SPAGHETTI ALLE VONGOLE

- Prep Time: 15 minutes
- Cook Time: 15 minutes
- Total Time: 30 minutes
- Servings: 4

Ingredients:

- 1 pound spaghetti
- 2 pounds fresh clams, scrubbed and rinsed
- 4 tablespoons olive oil
- 4 cloves garlic, minced
- 1/2 teaspoon red pepper flakes
- 1/2 cup dry white wine
- 1/4 cup chopped fresh parsley
- Salt, to taste
- Freshly ground black pepper, to taste
- Lemon wedges, for serving

Directions:

1. Cook the spaghetti pasta according to the package instructions until al dente. Remove the liquid and keep it aside.
2. Apply medium heat to the olive oil in a large skillet until it attains a warm temperature. Incorporate the minced garlic and red pepper flakes (if desired) into the skillet. Sauté for about 1 minute until the garlic becomes fragrant.
3. Add the clams to the skillet and pour in the white wine. Cover the skillet and cook for about 5-7 minutes, or until the clams open. Discard any clams that do not open.
4. Remove the cooked clams from the skillet and set aside. Keep the skillet with the clam cooking liquid on the heat.
5. Place the cooked spaghetti into the skillet containing the clam cooking liquid. Gently mix the pasta in the liquid to ensure even coating.
6. Introduce the diced fresh parsley to the skillet and season with desired amounts of salt and black pepper. Toss the pasta again to incorporate the ingredients.
7. Divide the spaghetti alle vongole among serving plates. Top each plate with the cooked clams.
8. Serve the Spaghetti alle Vongole hot, garnished with additional chopped parsley and lemon wedges on the side.

Nutritional Value per Serving:

Calories: 450 kcal, Protein: 20 grams, Carbohydrates: 70 grams, Fat: 10 grams, Saturated Fat: 1.5 grams, Cholesterol: 40 milligrams, Sodium: 300 milligrams, Fiber: 3 grams, and Sugar: 2 grams.

SEAFOOD FRA DIAVOLO

- Prep Time: 20 minutes
- Cook Time: 25 minutes
- Total Time: 45 minutes
- Servings: 4

Ingredients:

- 8 ounces linguine pasta
- 1 pound mixed seafood (shrimp, scallops, mussels, and/or clams)
- 2 tablespoons olive oil
- 4 cloves garlic, minced
- 1/2 teaspoon red pepper flakes
- 1 can (14 ounces) crushed tomatoes
- 1/2 cup dry white wine
- 1/4 cup chopped fresh basil
- Salt, to taste
- Freshly ground black pepper, to taste
- Fresh parsley, for garnish

Directions:

1. To achieve the desired al dente texture, cook the linguine pasta in accordance with the directions provided on the package. After cooking, remove the excess water from the pasta by draining it, and then set it aside for future use.
2. Take a large skillet and heat the olive oil over medium heat. Introduce the minced garlic and red pepper flakes to the skillet, and sauté them for approximately 1 minute until the garlic releases its aromatic fragrance.
3. Add the mixed seafood to the skillet and cook for about 2-3 minutes until they start to turn opaque.
4. Pour in the crushed tomatoes and white wine. Thoroughly blend the ingredients together to ensure they are fully combined, then proceed to bring the mixture to a gentle simmer. Let it cook for approximately 10 minutes, allowing the flavors to blend harmoniously.
5. Add the recently chopped basil into the skillet and customize the seasoning with salt and black pepper to suit your personal taste. Vigorously stir the mixture to ensure complete integration of all the ingredients.
6. Incorporate the cooked linguine pasta into the skillet and gently toss it with the sauce to evenly coat. Let it cook for an extra 2-3 minutes to ensure thorough heating.

7. Divide the Seafood Fra Diavolo among serving plates. Garnish with fresh parsley.

Nutritional Value per Serving:

Calories: 380 kcal, Protein: 30 grams, Carbohydrates: 40 grams, Fat: 10 grams, Saturated Fat: 1.5 grams, Cholesterol: 150 milligrams, Sodium: 600 milligrams, Fiber: 3 grams, and Sugar: 5 grams.

LINGUINE WITH LEMON GARLIC SHRIMP

- Prep Time: 15 minutes
- Cook Time: 15 minutes
- Total Time: 30 minutes
- Servings: 4

Ingredients:

- 8 ounces linguine pasta
- 1 pound shrimp, peeled and deveined
- 4 tablespoons butter
- 4 cloves garlic, minced
- 1/2 teaspoon red pepper flakes
- Zest of 1 lemon
- Juice of 1 lemon
- 1/4 cup chopped fresh parsley
- Salt, to taste
- Freshly ground black pepper, to taste
- Grated Parmesan cheese, for serving

Directions:

1. Prepare the linguine pasta by cooking it according to the instructions on the package until it reaches an al dente texture. After cooking the pasta, drain it and set it aside.
2. Start by heating the butter in a large skillet until it is fully melted. Next, introduce the minced garlic and red pepper flakes to the skillet. Sauté for about 1 minute until the garlic becomes fragrant.
3. Place the shrimp in the skillet and cook for approximately 2-3 minutes on each side until they become pink and opaque.
4. Add the lemon zest, lemon juice, and chopped fresh parsley to the skillet. Customize the seasoning by adding salt and black pepper to match your unique taste preferences. Stir to coat the shrimp evenly with the lemon garlic sauce.
5. Combine the cooked linguine pasta with the shrimp and sauce in the skillet, tossing them together. Heat for an extra 2-3 minutes to ensure everything is warmed through.
6. Divide the Linguine with Lemon Garlic Shrimp among serving plates. Serve hot, garnished with grated Parmesan cheese.

Nutritional Value per Serving:

Calories: 380 kcal, Protein: 25 grams, Carbohydrates: 40 grams, Fat: 12 grams, Saturated Fat: 6 grams, Cholesterol: 220 milligrams, Sodium: 400 milligrams, Fiber: 2 grams, and Sugar: 2 grams.

CALAMARI PASTA WITH TOMATO AND BASIL

- Prep Time: 15 minutes
- Cook Time: 20 minutes
- Total Time: 35 minutes
- Servings: 4

Ingredients:

- 8 ounces linguine or spaghetti pasta
- 1 lb calamari, sliced into rings after cleaning
- 2 tablespoons olive oil
- 4 cloves garlic, minced
- 1 can (14 ounces) diced tomatoes
- 1/4 cup tomato paste
- 1/4 cup chopped fresh basil
- Salt, to taste
- Freshly ground black pepper, to taste
- Grated Parmesan cheese, for serving

Directions:

1. To achieve the desired al dente texture, prepare the pasta by carefully following the instructions provided on the package. After cooking, drain the pasta and keep it aside for future use.
2. In a spacious skillet, warm the olive oil over medium heat. Introduce the minced garlic and sauté for approximately 1 minute until it becomes aromatic.
3. Add the mixed seafood to the skillet and cook for about 2-3 minutes until they are cooked through and opaque. Transfer the seafood from the skillet and place it aside, saving it for future use.
4. Combine the diced tomatoes and tomato paste into the mixture, stirring well. Customize the flavor by adding salt and black pepper to your taste. Let it simmer for approximately 10 minutes, allowing the flavors to blend harmoniously.
5. Incorporate the cooked pasta into the skillet and mix it with the calamari and tomato sauce until well combined. Cook for an extra 2-3 minutes to ensure it is heated thoroughly.
6. Take the skillet off the heat and gently mix in the freshly chopped basil.
7. Divide the Calamari Pasta with Tomato and Basil among serving plates. Serve hot, garnished with grated Parmesan cheese.

Nutritional Value per Serving:

Calories: 345 kcal, Protein: 26 grams, Carbohydrates: 42 grams, Fat: 8 grams, Saturated Fat: 1 grams, Cholesterol: 260 milligrams, Sodium: 430 milligrams, Fiber: 2 grams, and Sugar: 4 grams.

SEAFOOD LINGUINE WITH WHITE WINE SAUCE

- Prep Time: 15 minutes
- Cook Time: 20 minutes
- Total Time: 35 minutes
- Servings: 4

Ingredients:

- 8 ounces linguine pasta
- 1 pound mixed seafood (such as shrimp, scallops, and calamari), cleaned and deveined
- 2 tablespoons olive oil
- 4 cloves garlic, minced
- 1/2 cup dry white wine
- 1 cup seafood or vegetable broth
- 1 cup heavy cream
- 1/4 cup grated Parmesan cheese
- 1/4 cup chopped fresh parsley
- Salt, to taste
- Freshly ground black pepper, to taste
- Lemon wedges, for serving

Directions:

1. Cook the linguine pasta al dente according to package instructions. Once the pasta is cooked, remove it from heat, drain the water, and set it aside for future use.
2. Gradually increase the heat to medium and warm the olive oil in a spacious skillet. Add minced garlic and sauté for 1 minute until fragrant.
3. Add the mixed seafood to the skillet and cook for about 2-3 minutes until they are cooked through and opaque. Transfer the seafood from the skillet and place it aside, saving it for future use.
4. In the same skillet, pour in the white wine and cook for about 2 minutes to allow the alcohol to evaporate.
5. Add the seafood or vegetable broth to the skillet and bring it to a simmer. Cook for about 5 minutes to reduce the liquid slightly.
6. Stir in the heavy cream and grated Parmesan cheese. Cook for an additional 2-3 minutes until the sauce thickens.
7. Return the cooked seafood to the skillet and toss it with the sauce to combine. Keep cooking for an additional 2 minutes to make sure that the dish is heated evenly.

8. Add the cooked linguine pasta to the skillet and toss it with the seafood and sauce to combine. Cook for an additional 2 minutes to coat the pasta with the sauce.
9. Take the pan off the heat and carefully incorporate the freshly chopped parsley into the mixture. Adjust the seasoning of the mixture to your personal taste by adding salt and freshly ground black pepper.
10. Divide the Seafood Linguine with White Wine Sauce among serving plates. Serve hot, garnished with lemon wedges.

Nutritional Value per Serving:

Calories: 520 kcal, Protein: 30 grams, Carbohydrates: 40 grams, Fat: 26 grams, Saturated Fat: 12 grams, Cholesterol: 180 milligrams, Sodium: 420 milligrams, Fiber: 2 grams, and Sugar: 2 grams.

TAGLIATELLE WITH LOBSTER AND CHERRY TOMATOES

- Prep Time: 20 minutes
- Cook Time: 25 minutes
- Total Time: 45 minutes
- Servings: 4

Ingredients:

- 8 ounces tagliatelle pasta
- 1 pound lobster tails, cooked and meat removed from the shell
- 2 tablespoons olive oil
- 4 cloves garlic, minced
- 1 pint cherry tomatoes, halved
- 1/4 cup white wine
- 1/4 cup chicken or vegetable broth
- 1/4 cup chopped fresh basil
- Salt, to taste
- Freshly ground black pepper, to taste
- Grated Parmesan cheese, for serving

Directions:

1. Cook the tagliatelle pasta according to the package instructions until al dente. Drain and set aside.
2. In a spacious frying pan, warm the olive oil over medium heat. Include the finely minced garlic and cook for roughly 60 seconds until it fills the air with its delightful fragrance and releases its aromatic essence.
3. Add the cherry tomatoes to the skillet and cook for about 2-3 minutes until they start to soften and release their juices.
4. Gently pour the white wine and chicken or vegetable broth into the mixture. Allow it to simmer and continue cooking for approximately 5 minutes, allowing the liquid to slightly reduce.
5. Add the cooked lobster meat to the skillet and toss it with the tomatoes and sauce to combine. Allow it to simmer and continue cooking for approximately 5 minutes, allowing the liquid to slightly reduce.
6. Add the cooked tagliatelle pasta to the skillet and toss it with the lobster, tomatoes, and sauce to combine. Cook for an additional 2 minutes to coat the pasta with the sauce.

7. Take the pan off the heat and carefully incorporate the freshly chopped basil. Customize the flavor by adding salt and freshly ground black pepper to your liking..
8. Divide the Tagliatelle with Lobster and Cherry Tomatoes among serving plates. Serve hot, garnished with grated Parmesan cheese.

Nutritional Value per Serving:

Calories: 524 kcal, Protein: 29 grams, Carbohydrates: 61 grams, Fat: 17 grams, Saturated Fat: 6 grams, Cholesterol: 105 milligrams, Sodium: 405 milligrams, Fiber: 3 grams, and Sugar: 3 grams.

LINGUINE WITH SAFFRON AND SHRIMP

- Prep Time: 15 minutes
- Cooking Time: 20 minutes
- Total Time: 35 minutes
- Servings: 4

Ingredients:

- 400g linguine pasta
- 1/2 teaspoon saffron threads
- 2 tablespoons olive oil
- 4 cloves garlic, minced
- 1/2 teaspoon red pepper flakes (optional)
- 500g shrimp, peeled and deveined
- 1/2 cup dry white wine
- 1 cup chicken broth
- 1/2 cup heavy cream
- 1/4 cup grated Parmesan cheese
- Salt and pepper to taste
- Fresh parsley leaves for garnish

Directions:

1. To prepare the linguine pasta, follow the instructions on the package and cook it in a generously salted pot of boiling water. Once the pasta is cooked, carefully strain the water and set it aside for future use.
2. In a small bowl, mix the saffron threads and 2 tablespoons of warm water together, stirring until the saffron is completely dissolved. Keep the mixture aside for later use.
3. To start, heat the olive oil in a large skillet over medium heat. Once heated, add the minced garlic and red pepper flakes (if desired) to the skillet. Sauté the mixture for approximately 1 minute or until it becomes fragrant.
4. Introduce the shrimp into the skillet and cook for approximately 2-3 minutes on each side until they transform into a pink and opaque color. Transfer the shrimp from the skillet to a separate plate and keep it aside for future use.
5. In the skillet that was previously used, pour in the white wine and allow it to simmer for approximately 2 minutes, giving the alcohol a chance to evaporate.
6. Add the chicken broth and saffron mixture to the skillet and bring to a simmer. Let it cook for 2 minutes.

7. Lower the heat to a gentle simmer and carefully incorporate the heavy cream into the mixture, stirring it thoroughly. Let it simmer gently for 3-4 minutes until the sauce thickens slightly.
8. Place the cooked shrimp back into the skillet and gently mix them with the sauce until they are fully coated.
9. Add the cooked linguine pasta to the skillet and toss well to combine with the sauce.
10. Sprinkle the finely grated Parmesan cheese evenly over the pasta and season it with salt and pepper according to your personal taste preferences. Toss gently to combine.
11. Serve the Linguine with Saffron and Shrimp in individual bowls, garnished with fresh parsley leaves.

Nutritional Value per Serving:

Calories: 542 kcal, Protein: 36 grams, Carbohydrates: 61 grams, Fat: 16 grams, Saturated Fat: 6 grams, Cholesterol: 250 milligrams, Sodium: 748 milligrams, Fiber: 3 grams, and Sugar: 2 grams.

SEAFOOD PASTA PRIMAVERA

- Total Time: 40 minutes
- Cooking Time: 20 minutes
- Prep Time: 20 minutes
- Servings: 4

Ingredients:

- 8 ounces linguine pasta
- 1 tablespoon olive oil
- 1/2 pound shrimp, peeled and deveined
- 1/2 pound scallops
- 1/2 pound mussels, cleaned and debearded
- 1/2 cup white wine
- 2 tablespoons butter
- 4 cloves garlic, minced
- 1 cup cherry tomatoes, halved
- 1 cup asparagus, cut into 1-inch pieces
- 1/2 cup sliced bell peppers
- 1/2 cup sliced zucchini
- 1/2 cup sliced mushrooms
- 1 cup heavy cream
- 1/4 cup grated Parmesan cheese
- 1/4 cup chopped fresh basil
- Salt and pepper, to taste

Directions:

1. To prepare the linguine pasta, simply adhere to the guidelines provided on the package. After the pasta has been cooked to perfection, proceed to drain it and set it aside for later utilization.
2. In a generously sized skillet, warm the olive oil over medium-high heat. Introduce the shrimp, scallops, and mussels into the skillet. Cook the seafood for 2-3 minutes until the shrimp turn pink and the scallops are golden brown. Transfer the seafood from the skillet onto a separate dish and keep it aside for later use.
3. Place the white wine in the skillet and let it simmer for around 2 minutes until it reduces slightly.

4. To the skillet, introduce the butter and allow it to melt. Incorporate the minced garlic, stirring continuously, and let it cook for approximately 1 minute until it emits a fragrant aroma.
5. Add the cherry tomatoes, asparagus, bell peppers, zucchini, and mushrooms to the skillet. Cook the vegetables for a duration of 5 minutes until they reach a tender consistency.
6. Reduce the heat to medium-low and pour in the heavy cream. Bring to a gentle simmer.
7. Stir in the grated Parmesan cheese until melted and well combined.
8. Add the cooked linguine pasta and seafood to the skillet. Toss to coat in the creamy sauce and heat through.
9. To elevate the taste of the dish, evenly sprinkle a combination of salt and pepper, making sure to adjust the quantity based on your own unique flavor preferences.
10. Remove from heat and sprinkle with chopped basil.
11. Serve the Seafood Pasta Primavera immediately, and enjoy!

Nutritional Value per Serving:

Calories: 550 kcal, Protein: 29 grams, Carbohydrates: 50 grams, Fat: 26 grams, Saturated Fat: 8 grams, Cholesterol: 25 milligrams, Sodium: 500 milligrams, Fiber: 4 grams, and Sugar: 6 grams.

FETTUCCINE WITH CREAMY GARLIC SCALLOPS

- Total Time: 30 minutes
- Cooking Time: 10 minutes
- Prep Time: 15 minutes
- Servings: 4

Ingredients:

- 12 ounces fettuccine pasta
- 1 pound scallops
- 2 tablespoons butter
- 4 cloves garlic, minced
- 1 cup heavy cream
- 1/2 cup grated Parmesan cheese
- 1/4 cup chopped fresh parsley
- Salt and pepper, to taste

Directions:

1. Cook the fettuccine pasta according to the package instructions. Drain and set aside.
2. Pat dry the scallops with a paper towel and season with salt and pepper.
3. To begin, melt the butter in a large skillet over medium-high heat. Next, add the scallops and cook for approximately 2-3 minutes on each side until they turn a golden brown color. Finally, remove the scallops from the skillet and set them aside for later use.
4. In the same skillet, incorporate the minced garlic and sauté it for approximately one minute until it becomes aromatic and releases its pleasant fragrance.
5. To minimize the heat, adjust it to medium-low and carefully pour the heavy cream into the skillet. Allow it to come to a gentle simmer.
6. Incorporate the grated Parmesan cheese into the mixture and stir it consistently until it fully melts and achieves a smooth and uniform consistency.
7. Place the cooked fettuccine pasta into the skillet and gently mix it with the creamy garlic sauce until it is well coated.
8. Return the scallops to the skillet and gently toss them with the pasta.
9. Remove from heat and sprinkle with chopped parsley.
10. Serve the Fettuccine with Creamy Garlic Scallops immediately, and enjoy!

Nutritional Value per Serving:

Calories: 560 kcal, Protein: 31 grams, Carbohydrates: 47 grams, Fat: 29 grams, Saturated Fat: 10 grams, Cholesterol: 35 milligrams, Sodium: 480 milligrams, Fiber: 2 grams, and Sugar: 2 grams.

CHAPTER 8: VEGETARIAN AND VEGAN PASTA DISHES

VEGAN PASTA PRIMAVERA

- Total Cooking Time: 25 minutes
- Prep Time: 15 minutes
- Servings: 4

Ingredients:

- 8 ounces of fettuccine pasta (vegan, if desired)
- 2 tablespoons olive oil
- 1 small onion, thinly sliced
- 2 cloves of garlic, minced
- 1 medium zucchini, sliced
- 1 medium yellow squash, sliced
- 1 red bell pepper, sliced
- 1 cup cherry tomatoes, halved
- 1 cup fresh or frozen peas
- 1 cup vegetable broth
- 1 teaspoon dried basil
- 1 teaspoon dried oregano
- Salt and pepper, to taste
- Vegan parmesan cheese, for garnish (optional)
- Fresh basil leaves, for garnish (optional)

Directions:

1. Cook the fettuccine pasta according to the package instructions. Once cooked, drain and set aside.
2. Begin by pouring the olive oil into a spacious skillet and heating it over medium heat until it reaches the desired temperature. Next, introduce the onion and garlic into the skillet, sautéing them until the onion takes on a translucent appearance.
3. Add the zucchini, yellow squash, red bell pepper, cherry tomatoes, and peas to the skillet. Cook for about 5 minutes, until the vegetables are tender-crisp.
4. Start by carefully pouring the vegetable broth into the mixture, then add the dried basil and oregano. Customize the seasoning with salt and pepper to match your individual flavor preferences. Vigorously mix the contents to ensure they are thoroughly blended together.
5. Add the cooked fettuccine pasta to the skillet and toss until well coated with the vegetable mixture. Extend the simmering time of the mixture by 2-3 minutes to enable the flavors to combine and form a cohesive and balanced blend.

6. Remove from heat and serve the Fettuccine with Vegan Pasta Primavera hot. If desired, top with vegan parmesan cheese and fresh basil leaves for an added touch of flavor and presentation.

Nutritional Value per Serving:

Calories: 350 kcal, Protein: 12 grams, Carbohydrates: 55 grams, Fat: 10 grams, Saturated Fat: 1.5 grams, Cholesterol: 0 milligrams, Sodium: 300 milligrams, Fiber: 8 grams, and Sugar: 9 grams.

EGGPLANT AND TOMATO PASTA

- Total Cooking Time: 35 minutes
- Prep Time: 15 minutes
- Servings: 4

Ingredients:

- 8 ounces of pasta
- 2 tablespoons olive oil
- 1 medium eggplant, diced
- 1 small onion, finely chopped
- 2 cloves of garlic, minced
- 2 cups cherry tomatoes, halved
- 1 teaspoon dried basil
- 1 teaspoon dried oregano
- 1/2 teaspoon red pepper flakes
- Salt and pepper, to taste
- Fresh basil leaves, for garnish (optional)
- Vegan parmesan cheese, for garnish (optional)

Directions:

1. Prepare the pasta as per the instructions on the package. After cooking, strain the pasta and keep it aside for later use.
2. To warm the olive oil, simply utilize a spacious skillet set to medium heat. Add the diced eggplant and cook for approximately 5 minutes until it begins to soften and becomes tender.
3. To the skillet, include the finely chopped onion and minced garlic. Sauté until the onion turns translucent.
4. Add the cherry tomatoes to the skillet and cook for another 5 minutes, until they start to release their juices.
5. Sprinkle the dried basil, dried oregano, red pepper flakes (if using), salt, and pepper over the vegetables. Stir well to combine.
6. Continue cooking for about 10 minutes, until the eggplant is tender and the flavors have melded together.
7. Combine the cooked pasta with the vegetable mixture in the skillet, ensuring that it is thoroughly coated. Continue cooking for an extra 2 to 3 minutes to give the flavors a chance to meld together.

8. Remove from heat and serve the Eggplant and Tomato Pasta hot. To enhance the presentation, you have the option to top it off with fresh basil leaves and vegan parmesan cheese.

Nutritional Value per Serving:

Calories: 350 kcal, Protein: 10 grams, Carbohydrates: 60 grams, Fat: 4 grams, Saturated Fat: 1 grams, Cholesterol: 0 milligrams, Sodium: 200 milligrams, Fiber: 10 grams, and Sugar: 8 grams.

MEDITERRANEAN ORZO SALAD

- Total Cooking Time: 20 minutes
- Prep Time: 10 minutes
- Servings: 4

Ingredients:

- 8 ounces of orzo pasta
- 1 cup cherry tomatoes, halved
- 1 cup cucumber, diced
- 1/2 cup pitted Kalamata olives, halved
- 1/2 cup red onion, finely chopped
- 1/2 cup crumbled feta cheese
- 1/4 cup fresh basil leaves, chopped
- 2 tablespoons extra virgin olive oil
- 2 tablespoons lemon juice
- 1 clove garlic, minced
- Salt and pepper, to taste

Directions:

1. To prepare the orzo pasta, follow the instructions on the package. After cooking the pasta, it is advisable to drain it and give it a thorough rinse with cold water to cool it down.
2. In a spacious bowl, mix together the cooked orzo pasta, cherry tomatoes, cucumber, Kalamata olives, red onion, crumbled feta cheese, and fresh basil leaves, ensuring that all the ingredients are well incorporated.
3. To create the dressing, combine extra virgin olive oil, lemon juice, minced garlic, salt, and pepper in a small bowl. Combine the ingredients and thoroughly mix them until they are fully blended and incorporated.
4. Pour the dressing evenly over the orzo salad and gently toss it to ensure that all the ingredients are coated with the dressing and well combined.
5. Taste the dish and make any necessary adjustments to the seasoning, if desired.
6. Serve the Mediterranean Orzo Salad chilled or at room temperature.

Nutritional Value per Serving:

Calories: 320 kcal, Protein: 9 grams, Carbohydrates: 45 grams, Fat: 12 grams, Saturated Fat: 4 grams, Cholesterol: 15 milligrams, Sodium: 450 milligrams, Fiber: 3 grams, and Sugar: 4 grams.

CAPRESE PASTA SALAD

- Total Cooking Time: 20 minutes
- Prep Time: 10 minutes
- Servings: 4

Ingredients:

- 8 ounces of pasta
- 1 cup cherry tomatoes, halved
- 8 ounces fresh mozzarella cheese, diced
- 1/4 cup fresh basil leaves, torn
- 2 tablespoons extra virgin olive oil
- 2 tablespoons balsamic vinegar
- Salt and pepper, to taste

Directions:

1. For proper preparation of the pasta, it is recommended to consult the instructions provided on the packaging as a starting point. Once it is cooked, carefully drain the pasta and rinse it with cold water to bring down its temperature.
2. Take a spacious bowl and mix together the cooked pasta, cherry tomatoes, fresh mozzarella cheese, and torn basil leaves.
3. Combine the extra virgin olive oil, balsamic vinegar, salt, and pepper in a small bowl, whisking them vigorously until they blend harmoniously to form a delectable and impeccably seasoned dressing.
4. With caution, drizzle the dressing evenly over the pasta salad, gently incorporating it to ensure that each ingredient is fully coated with the dressing.
5. Sample the dish and, if desired, make any required modifications to the seasoning.
6. Serve the Caprese Pasta Salad chilled or at room temperature.

Nutritional Value per Serving:

Calories: 380 kcal, Protein: 16 grams, Carbohydrates: 38 grams, Fat: 18 grams, Saturated Fat: 4 grams, Cholesterol: 30 milligrams, Sodium: 350 milligrams, Fiber: 2 grams, and Sugar: 3 grams.

VEGAN PASTA PUTTANESCA

- Total Cooking Time: 25 minutes
- Prep Time: 10 minutes
- Servings: 4

Ingredients:

- 8 ounces of pasta
- 2 tablespoons olive oil
- 3 cloves garlic, minced
- 1 small onion, finely chopped
- 1 can (14 ounces) diced tomatoes
- 1/4 cup pitted Kalamata olives, halved
- 2 tablespoons capers
- 1 teaspoon dried oregano
- 1/2 teaspoon red pepper flakes
- Salt and pepper, to taste
- Fresh parsley, chopped (for garnish)

Directions:

1. Get the pasta ready by carefully following the instructions provided on the package. Once cooked to perfection, drain the pasta and set it aside for later use.
2. Using a large skillet, heat up the olive oil over medium heat. Next, incorporate the minced garlic and chopped onion into the skillet, sautéing them until the onion turns translucent and the garlic emits its delightful aroma.
3. Combine the diced tomatoes, Kalamata olives, capers, dried oregano, and red pepper flakes in the skillet, ensuring they are fully integrated into the mixture. Stir thoroughly to ensure all the ingredients are well combined.
4. Reduce the heat to low and let the sauce simmer for about 10 minutes, allowing the flavors to meld together. Season with salt and pepper to taste.
5. Incorporate the cooked pasta into the skillet and gently toss it to ensure it is well coated with the sauce.
6. Cook for an additional 2-3 minutes, until the pasta is heated through.
7. Serve the Vegan Pasta Puttanesca garnished with fresh parsley.

Nutritional Value per Serving:

Calories: 350 kcal, Protein: 10 grams, Carbohydrates: 55 grams, Fat: 10 grams, Saturated Fat: 4 grams, Cholesterol: 15 milligrams, Sodium: 600 milligrams, Fiber: 5 grams, and Sugar: 5 grams.

VEGAN PASTA WITH ROASTED RED PEPPER SAUCE

- Total Cooking Time: 40 minutes
- Prep Time: 15 minutes
- Servings: 4

Ingredients:

- 8 ounces of pasta
- 2 red bell peppers
- 1 tablespoon olive oil
- 1 small onion, diced
- 3 cloves of garlic, minced
- 1 can (14 ounces) diced tomatoes
- 1/4 cup tomato paste
- 1 teaspoon dried basil
- 1 teaspoon dried oregano
- 1/2 teaspoon red pepper flakes
- Salt and pepper, to taste
- Fresh basil leaves, chopped (for garnish)

Directions:

1. To get started, make sure your oven is preheated to a temperature of 450°F (230°C). To get the red bell peppers ready, simply arrange them on a baking sheet and let them roast in the oven for roughly 20 minutes, or until the skins become charred and blistered. Remove from the oven and let them cool slightly. Once cooled, remove the skins, seeds, and stems, and roughly chop the roasted peppers.
2. Follow the instructions on the pasta package to cook it. Once it's done, drain the pasta and set it aside.
3. In a large skillet, heat the olive oil over medium heat. Add the diced onion and minced garlic, and sauté until the onion is translucent and the garlic is fragrant.
4. Add the roasted red peppers, diced tomatoes, tomato paste, dried basil, dried oregano, and red pepper flakes to the skillet. Stir well to combine.
5. Reduce the heat to low and let the sauce simmer for about 10 minutes, allowing the flavors to meld together. Season with salt and pepper to taste.
6. To achieve a smooth consistency, transfer the sauce to a blender or employ an immersion blender to blend it thoroughly.

7. Return the sauce to the skillet and add the cooked pasta. To guarantee that the pasta is evenly coated with the sauce, delicately mix them together and keep cooking for an extra 2-3 minutes until the pasta is fully heated.
8. Serve the Vegan Pasta with Roasted Red Pepper Sauce garnished with fresh basil leaves.

Nutritional Value per Serving:

Calories: 320 kcal, Protein: 10 grams, Carbohydrates: 60 grams, Fat: 5 grams, Saturated Fat: 1 grams, Cholesterol: 20 milligrams, Sodium: 350 milligrams, Fiber: 6 grams, and Sugar: 8 grams.

LEMON GARLIC SPAGHETTI

- Total Cooking Time: 20 minutes
- Prep Time: 10 minutes
- Servings: 4

Ingredients:

- 8 ounces of spaghetti
- 4 tablespoons butter
- 4 cloves of garlic, minced
- Zest of 1 lemon
- Juice of 1 lemon
- 1/4 cup grated Parmesan cheese
- Salt and pepper, to taste
- Fresh parsley, chopped (for garnish)

Directions:

1. Simply adhere to the guidelines provided on the spaghetti packaging to properly cook it. After it has been cooked, drain the spaghetti and set it aside for future use.
2. Take a generously sized skillet and heat the butter over medium heat. Then, introduce the minced garlic and cook it for about 1-2 minutes until it emanates a delightful aroma.
3. Afterward, add the lemon zest and lemon juice to the skillet, making sure to stir diligently to achieve a thorough and even mixture.
4. Add the cooked spaghetti to the skillet and toss to coat the pasta with the lemon garlic sauce.
5. Cook for an additional 2-3 minutes, until the pasta is heated through.
6. Once removed from the heat, gently incorporate the grated Parmesan cheese into the mixture. Remember to season with salt and pepper according to your taste preferences.
7. Serve the Lemon Garlic Spaghetti garnished with fresh parsley.

Nutritional Value per Serving:

Calories: 350 kcal, Protein: 10 grams, Carbohydrates: 50 grams, Fat: 12 grams, Saturated Fat: 7 grams, Cholesterol: 20 milligrams, Sodium: 200 milligrams, Fiber: 2 grams, and Sugar: 2 grams.

MEDITERRANEAN PASTA WITH ARTICHOKES AND SUN-DRIED TOMATOES

- Total Cooking Time: 30 minutes
- Prep Time: 10 minutes
- Servings: 4

Ingredients:

- 8 ounces of pasta
- 2 tablespoons olive oil
- 3 cloves of garlic, minced
- 1 can (14 ounces) artichoke hearts, drained and quartered
- 1/2 cup sun-dried tomatoes, chopped
- 1/4 cup Kalamata olives, pitted and halved
- 1/4 cup fresh basil leaves, chopped
- 1/4 cup grated Parmesan cheese
- Salt and pepper, to taste

Directions:

1. To prepare the pasta, just adhere to the guidelines given on the packaging. Once it is thoroughly cooked, drain the pasta and set it aside for future use.
2. Begin by heating olive oil in a large skillet over medium heat. Proceed to add minced garlic and sauté it for 1-2 minutes until it becomes fragrant.
3. Add the artichoke hearts, sun-dried tomatoes, and Kalamata olives to the skillet. Thoroughly mix the ingredients together and continue cooking for an extra 3-4 minutes until they are heated through.
4. Incorporate the cooked pasta into the skillet and gently mix it with the mixture until it is well coated. Allow it to cook for an extra 2-3 minutes, enabling the flavors to blend harmoniously.
5. Take the skillet off the heat and incorporate the chopped basil leaves. Sprinkle a small amount of salt and pepper based on your personal taste.
6. Serve the Mediterranean Pasta with Artichokes and Sun-Dried Tomatoes garnished with grated Parmesan cheese.

Nutritional Value per Serving:

Calories: 380 kcal, Protein: 10 grams, Carbohydrates: 58 grams, Fat: 12 grams, Saturated Fat: 4=2 grams, Cholesterol: 12 milligrams, Sodium: 450 milligrams, Fiber: 5 grams, and Sugar: 10 grams.

VEGAN PESTO PASTA

- Total Cooking Time: 20 minutes
- Prep Time: 10 minutes
- Servings: 4

Ingredients:

- 8 ounces of pasta
- 2 cups fresh basil leaves
- 1/2 cup pine nuts
- 3 cloves of garlic
- 1/4 cup nutritional yeast
- 1/4 cup extra virgin olive oil
- 1 tablespoon lemon juice
- Salt and pepper, to taste
- Optional toppings: cherry tomatoes, sliced olives, chopped fresh basil

Directions:

1. To cook the pasta, simply follow the instructions provided on the packaging. Once it is cooked to perfection, drain the pasta and set it aside for later use.
2. Combine the basil leaves, pine nuts, garlic, nutritional yeast, olive oil, lemon juice, salt, and pepper in a food processor or blender. Blend the ingredients until they create a silky and creamy consistency.
3. Combine the cooked pasta and pesto sauce in a large mixing bowl. Toss the mixture well to ensure that the pasta is evenly coated with the flavorful sauce.
4. Optional: Add cherry tomatoes, sliced olives, or chopped fresh basil as desired for additional flavor and texture.
5. Serve the Vegan Pesto Pasta immediately and enjoy!

Nutritional Value per Serving:

Calories: 400 kcal, Protein: 10 grams, Carbohydrates: 45 grams, Fat: 20 grams, Saturated Fat: 2 grams, Cholesterol: 12 milligrams, Sodium: 150 milligrams, Fiber: 5 grams, and Sugar: 2 grams.

GREEK PASTA SALAD

- Total Cooking Time: 20 minutes
- Prep Time: 10 minutes
- Servings: 6

Ingredients:

- 8 ounces of pasta
- 1 cup cherry tomatoes, halved
- 1 cup cucumber, diced
- 1/2 cup Kalamata olives, pitted and halved
- 1/2 cup red onion, thinly sliced
- 1/2 cup crumbled feta cheese
- 1/4 cup fresh parsley, chopped
- 1/4 cup fresh dill, chopped
- 1/4 cup extra virgin olive oil
- 2 tablespoons red wine vinegar
- 1 clove garlic, minced
- Salt and pepper, to taste

Directions:

1. To make the pasta, carefully follow the instructions on the packaging. After the pasta has cooked to the desired level of doneness, carefully drain it and then give it a revitalizing rinse using cold water. This will help cool it down and ensure it doesn't overcook.
2. In a spacious mixing bowl, mix together the cooked pasta, cherry tomatoes, cucumber, Kalamata olives, red onion, feta cheese, parsley, and dill. Combine all the ingredients thoroughly to create a delicious and refreshing pasta salad.
3. Combine the olive oil, red wine vinegar, minced garlic, salt, and pepper in a small bowl. Vigorously whisk the ingredients together until they meld together seamlessly, resulting in a delectable dressing bursting with flavor.
4. Drizzle the dressing over the pasta salad and mix thoroughly to ensure all the ingredients are evenly coated.
5. Sample the dish and modify the seasoning with salt and pepper as necessary to achieve the desired taste.
6. Serve the Greek Pasta Salad chilled or at room temperature.

Nutritional Value per Serving:

Calories: 320 kcal, Protein: 9 grams, Carbohydrates: 38 grams, Fat: 15 grams, Saturated Fat: 4 grams, Cholesterol: 10 milligrams, Sodium: 380 milligrams, Fiber: 3 grams, and Sugar: 3 grams.

CHAPTER 9:
MEDITERRANEAN
PASTA SALADS

CLASSIC GREEK PASTA SALAD

- Prep Time: 15 minutes
- Cooking Time: 10 minutes
- Total Time: 25 minutes
- Servings: 4

Ingredients:

- 8 ounces (225g) rotini pasta
- 1 cup cherry tomatoes, halved
- 1 cucumber, diced
- 1/2 red onion, thinly sliced
- 1/2 cup pitted Kalamata olives, halved
- 1/2 cup crumbled feta cheese
- 1/4 cup fresh parsley, chopped
- 1/4 cup fresh dill, chopped

For the Dressing:

- 1/4 cup extra virgin olive oil
- 2 tablespoons red wine vinegar
- 1 clove garlic, minced
- 1 teaspoon dried oregano
- Salt and pepper to taste

Directions:

1. In a generously-sized mixing bowl, gently combine the cooked pasta, cherry tomatoes, cucumber, red onion, Kalamata olives, feta cheese, parsley, and dill, ensuring all the ingredients are evenly distributed.
2. In a large mixing bowl, combine the cooked pasta, cherry tomatoes, cucumber, red onion, Kalamata olives, feta cheese, parsley, and dill.
3. To prepare the dressing, combine the olive oil, red wine vinegar, minced garlic, dried oregano, salt, and pepper in a small mixing bowl. Whisk the ingredients vigorously until they are well blended, resulting in a flavorful dressing.
4. Once the dressing is ready, drizzle it generously over the pasta salad, ensuring that each component receives an even coating. To combine the flavors, delicately toss the salad, allowing the dressing to blend seamlessly with the ingredients.

5. For enhanced flavors and a harmonious blend, cover and refrigerate the salad for at least one hour. This melding of ingredients during the cooling period creates a delicious and well-balanced dish that is more flavorful and enjoyable.

6. Before serving, give the salad a final toss and adjust the seasoning if needed.

Nutritional breakdown per serving:

Calories: 354 kcal, Protein: 9 grams, Carbohydrates: 34 grams, Fat: 20 grams, Saturated Fat: 2 grams, Cholesterol: 23 milligrams, Sodium: 575 milligrams, Fiber: 3 grams, and Sugar: 4 grams.

MEDITERRANEAN ORZO SALAD

- Prep Time: 15 minutes
- Cooking Time: 10 minutes
- Total Time: 25 minutes
- Servings: 4

Ingredients:

- 1 cup orzo pasta
- 1 cup cherry tomatoes, halved
- 1/2 cup cucumber, diced
- 1/2 cup Kalamata olives, pitted and halved
- 1/4 cup red onion, finely chopped
- 1/4 cup crumbled feta cheese
- 1/4 cup fresh parsley, chopped
- 2 tablespoons fresh mint leaves, chopped

For the Dressing:

- 3 tablespoons extra virgin olive oil
- 2 tablespoons lemon juice
- 1 clove garlic, minced
- 1/2 teaspoon dried oregano
- Salt and pepper to taste

Directions:

1. To prepare the orzo pasta, follow the instructions on the package and cook it until it reaches the desired al dente texture. After the pasta is cooked, proceed to drain it and rinse it thoroughly with cold water in order to cool it down..
2. In a big bowl, mix cooked orzo, cherry tomatoes, cucumber, Kalamata olives, red onion, feta cheese, parsley, and mint leaves.
3. To prepare the dressing, combine olive oil, lemon juice, minced garlic, dried oregano, salt, and pepper in a small bowl. Whisk the ingredients until they are fully mixed together.
4. Pour the dressing over the orzo salad and toss gently until well coated.
5. Once you have covered the salad, place it in the refrigerator for at least one hour to allow the flavors to blend together.
6. Before serving, give the salad a final toss and adjust the seasoning if needed.

Nutritional breakdown per serving:

Calories: 258 kcal, Protein: 7 grams, Carbohydrates: 30 grams, Fat: 12 grams, Saturated Fat: 4 grams, Cholesterol: 25 milligrams, Sodium: 410 milligrams, Fiber: 3 grams, and Sugar: 2 grams.

ITALIAN CAPRESE PASTA SALAD

- Total Cooking Time: 15 minutes
- Prep Time: 10 minutes
- Servings: 4

Ingredients:

- 8 ounces penne pasta
- 1 cup cherry tomatoes, halved
- 8 ounces fresh mozzarella cheese, cubed
- 1/4 cup fresh basil leaves, torn
- 2 tablespoons extra virgin olive oil
- 2 tablespoons balsamic vinegar
- Salt and pepper to taste

Directions:

1. To prepare the penne pasta, carefully follow the instructions provided on the packaging until it reaches the desired level of firmness, commonly referred to as "al dente." Once the pasta is cooked to perfection, gently drain it and give it a thorough rinse with cold water to quickly cool it down.
2. In a large mixing bowl, combine the penne pasta (cooked and cooled), cherry tomatoes, fresh mozzarella cheese, and torn basil leaves. Gently mix all the ingredients together to create a flavorful and colorful dish.
3. In a small bowl, vigorously combine the extra virgin olive oil, balsamic vinegar, salt, and pepper. Whisk the ingredients together until they blend seamlessly, resulting in a perfectly balanced mixture.
4. Drizzle the dressing onto the pasta salad and toss delicately to ensure all the ingredients are coated evenly.
5. Take a moment to taste the dish and make any necessary adjustments to the seasoning, if desired.
6. You have the option to either serve the Italian Caprese Pasta Salad immediately or refrigerate it for a few hours, enabling the flavors to meld together in perfect harmony.

Nutritional breakdown per serving:

Calories: 360 kcal, Protein: 15 grams, Carbohydrates: 35 grams, Fat: 18 grams, Saturated Fat: 7 grams, Cholesterol: 35 milligrams, Sodium: 280 milligrams, Fiber: 2 grams, and Sugar: 3 grams.

LEMON HERB COUSCOUS SALAD

- Total Cooking Time: 20 minutes
- Prep Time: 10 minutes
- Servings: 4

Ingredients:

- 1 cup couscous
- 1 ¼ cups vegetable broth
- 2 tablespoons olive oil
- 1 tablespoon lemon juice
- 2 teaspoons lemon zest
- 1 tablespoon fresh parsley, chopped
- 1 tablespoon fresh mint, chopped
- 1 tablespoon fresh dill, chopped
- 1 cucumber, diced
- 1 red bell pepper, diced
- 1 cup cherry tomatoes, halved
- ¼ cup red onion, finely chopped
- Salt and pepper to taste

Directions:

1. In a medium-sized saucepan, heat the vegetable broth until it reaches a boiling point. Once it starts boiling, take it off the heat and mix in the couscous. Cover the saucepan and let it sit for about 5 minutes, or until the couscous has absorbed all the liquid.
2. After cooking, use a fork to fluff the couscous and then transfer it to a spacious mixing bowl.
3. In a separate small bowl, thoroughly whisk together the olive oil, lemon juice, lemon zest, parsley, mint, dill, salt, and pepper, ensuring all the ingredients are well combined.
4. Pour the dressing over the couscous and toss to coat.
5. Add the cucumber, red bell pepper, cherry tomatoes, and red onion to the couscous mixture. Carefully mix the ingredients together until they are thoroughly combined.
6. Test the flavor and make any necessary adjustments to the seasoning.
7. You have two options for the Lemon Herb Couscous Salad: either serve it immediately or refrigerate it for a few hours to allow the flavors to combine and enhance.

Nutritional breakdown per serving:

Calories: 220 kcal, Protein: 5 grams, Carbohydrates: 33 grams, Fat: 8 grams, Saturated Fat: 1 grams, Cholesterol: 0 milligrams, Sodium: 350 milligrams, Fiber: 4 grams, and Sugar: 4 grams.

MEDITERRANEAN PASTA SALAD WITH TZATZIKI DRESSING

- Total Cooking Time: 20 minutes
- Prep Time: 10 minutes
- Servings: 4

Ingredients:

For the Mediterranean Pasta Salad:

- 8 ounces rotini pasta
- 1 cup cherry tomatoes, halved
- 1 cucumber, diced
- 1/2 red onion, thinly sliced
- 1/2 cup Kalamata olives, pitted and halved
- 1/2 cup crumbled feta cheese
- 1/4 cup fresh parsley, chopped
- 1/4 cup fresh basil, chopped

For the Tzatziki Dressing:

- 1 cup Greek yogurt
- 1/4 cup cucumber, grated and squeezed to remove excess moisture
- 1 clove garlic, minced
- 1 tablespoon lemon juice
- 1 tablespoon extra virgin olive oil
- 1 tablespoon fresh dill, chopped
- Salt and pepper to taste

Directions:

1. To get the rotini pasta ready, make sure to follow the instructions provided on the package until it reaches the desired al dente texture. Once it's cooked to perfection, drain the pasta and give it a refreshing rinse with cold water to cool it down.
2. To make the dish, take a large mixing bowl and add the cooked and cooled rotini pasta along with cherry tomatoes, cucumber, red onion, Kalamata olives, feta cheese, parsley, and basil. Gently combine all the ingredients together in the bowl.

3. To prepare the dressing, take a separate small bowl and whisk together Greek yogurt, grated cucumber, minced garlic, lemon juice, olive oil, fresh dill, salt, and pepper until thoroughly combined.
4. After preparing the tzatziki dressing, pour it over the pasta salad and carefully toss the ingredients to ensure they are evenly coated.
5. Feel free to taste the dish and make any necessary adjustments to the seasoning, if desired.
6. Serve the Mediterranean Pasta Salad with Tzatziki Dressing immediately or refrigerate for a few hours to let the flavors meld together.

Nutritional breakdown per serving:

Calories: 320 kcal, Protein: 14 grams, Carbohydrates: 45 grams, Fat: 10 grams, Saturated Fat: 4 grams, Cholesterol: 20 milligrams, Sodium: 520 milligrams, Fiber: 4 grams, and Sugar: 6 grams.

ROASTED VEGETABLE PASTA SALAD

- Total Cooking Time: 40 minutes
- Prep Time: 15 minutes
- Servings: 4

Ingredients:

- 8 ounces rotini pasta
- 1 red bell pepper, sliced
- 1 yellow bell pepper, sliced
- 1 zucchini, sliced
- 1 yellow squash, sliced
- 1 cup cherry tomatoes, halved
- 1/4 cup red onion, thinly sliced
- 2 tablespoons olive oil
- 2 cloves garlic, minced
- 1 teaspoon dried Italian seasoning
- Salt and pepper to taste
- 1/4 cup fresh basil, chopped
- 1/4 cup grated Parmesan cheese

Directions:

1. To start the cooking process, it is important to preheat the oven to 425°F (220°C) to make sure it reaches the necessary temperature before continuing with the recipe.
2. Cook the rotini pasta according to package instructions until al dente. Drain and set aside.
3. In a large baking sheet, combine the sliced red and yellow bell peppers, zucchini, yellow squash, cherry tomatoes, and red onion.
4. In a compact bowl, combine the olive oil, minced garlic, dried Italian seasoning, salt, and pepper. Proceed to drizzle this mixture over the vegetables and toss them gently to ensure an even coating.
5. Roast the vegetables in the preheated oven for about 20-25 minutes, or until they are tender and slightly caramelized. Stir the vegetables halfway through cooking for even browning.
6. In a spacious mixing bowl, unite the cooked rotini pasta and roasted vegetables. Introduce the chopped fresh basil and grated Parmesan cheese. Gently toss the ingredients together until they are well combined.

7. To ensure the desired flavor, take a small sample and make any necessary adjustments to the seasoning.
8. Serve the Roasted Vegetable Pasta Salad warm or at room temperature.

Nutritional breakdown per serving:

Calories: 320 kcal, Protein: 10 grams, Carbohydrates: 50 grams, Fat: 10 grams, Saturated Fat: 2 grams, Cholesterol: 5 milligrams, Sodium: 150 milligrams, Fiber: 5 grams, and Sugar: 6 grams.

MEDITERRANEAN PASTA SALAD WITH SUN-DRIED TOMATO PESTO

- Total Cooking Time: 25 minutes
- Prep Time: 15 minutes
- Servings: 4

Ingredients:

For the Mediterranean Pasta Salad:

- 8 ounces fusilli pasta
- 1 cup cherry tomatoes, halved
- 1/2 cup sliced black olives
- 1/2 cup diced cucumber
- 1/4 cup diced red onion
- 1/4 cup crumbled feta cheese
- 2 tablespoons chopped fresh basil
- 2 tablespoons chopped fresh parsley

For the Sun-Dried Tomato Pesto:

- 1/2 cup sun-dried tomatoes (drained, in oil)
- 1/4 cup grated Parmesan cheese
- 2 tablespoons pine nuts
- 2 cloves garlic
- 1/4 cup extra virgin olive oil
- Salt and pepper to taste

Directions:

1. To achieve the desired texture, refer to the instructions on the package for cooking the fusilli pasta until it is al dente. After cooking, proceed to drain the pasta and use cold water to cool it down.

2. In a generously sized mixing bowl, merge the cooked and cooled fusilli pasta with cherry tomatoes, black olives, cucumber, red onion, feta cheese, basil, and parsley.

3. Utilizing a food processor or blender, combine the sun-dried tomatoes, grated Parmesan cheese, pine nuts, garlic, olive oil, salt, and pepper. Blend the components until they form a silky and completely blended concoction.

4. Pour the sun-dried tomato pesto over the pasta salad and toss gently to coat all the ingredients.

5. Sample the dish and make any necessary adjustments to the seasoning according to your preference.

6. Serve the Mediterranean Pasta Salad with Sun-Dried Tomato Pesto immediately or refrigerate for a few hours to let the flavors meld together.

Nutritional breakdown per serving:

Calories: 380 kcal, Protein: 10 grams, Carbohydrates: 45 grams, Fat: 18 grams, Saturated Fat: 4 grams, Cholesterol: 10 milligrams, Sodium: 420 milligrams, Fiber: 4 grams, and Sugar: 4 grams.

MEDITERRANEAN PASTA SALAD WITH ARTICHOKES AND CHICKPEAS

- Total Cooking Time: 20 minutes
- Prep Time: 10 minutes
- Servings: 4

Ingredients:

- 8 ounces fusilli pasta
- 1 can (14 ounces) artichoke hearts, drained and quartered
- 1 can (14 ounces) chickpeas, drained and rinsed
- 1 cup cherry tomatoes, halved
- 1/2 cup sliced black olives
- 1/4 cup diced red onion
- 1/4 cup crumbled feta cheese
- 2 tablespoons chopped fresh parsley
- 2 tablespoons lemon juice
- 2 tablespoons extra virgin olive oil
- Salt and pepper to taste

Directions:

1. For a successful preparation of fusilli pasta, it is essential to follow the instructions given on the packaging and cook it until it reaches the desired al dente texture. Following the cooking process, drain the pasta and proceed to cool it down by giving it a thorough rinse with cold water.
2. In a spacious mixing bowl, blend together the cooked and cooled fusilli pasta, artichoke hearts, chickpeas, cherry tomatoes, black olives, red onion, feta cheese, and parsley.
3. In a small bowl, combine the lemon juice, extra virgin olive oil, salt, and pepper. Stir with passion and vigor to ensure a complete and thorough mixing of the ingredients.
4. Drizzle the dressing over the pasta salad and delicately toss to evenly coat all of the ingredients.
5. Sample the dish and make any necessary adjustments to the seasoning based on your taste preferences.
6. Serve the Mediterranean Pasta Salad with Artichokes and Chickpeas immediately or refrigerate for a few hours to let the flavors meld together.

Nutritional breakdown per serving:

Calories: 380 kcal, Protein: 14 grams, Carbohydrates: 55 grams, Fat: 12 grams, Saturated Fat: 2 grams, Cholesterol: 5 milligrams, Sodium: 580 milligrams, Fiber: 9 grams, and Sugar: 4 grams.

MEDITERRANEAN PASTA SALAD WITH BALSAMIC VINAIGRETTE

- Total Cooking Time: 20 minutes
- Prep Time: 10 minutes
- Servings: 4

Ingredients:

<u>For the Salad:</u>

- 8 ounces rotini or penne pasta
- 1 cup cherry tomatoes, halved
- 1 cup cucumber, diced
- 1/2 cup Kalamata olives, pitted and halved
- 1/2 cup red onion, thinly sliced
- 1/2 cup crumbled feta cheese
- 1/4 cup fresh basil leaves, chopped
- 1/4 cup fresh parsley leaves, chopped

<u>For the Balsamic Vinaigrette:</u>

- 1/4 cup balsamic vinegar
- 2 tablespoons extra virgin olive oil
- 1 tablespoon Dijon mustard
- 1 clove garlic, minced
- 1 teaspoon dried oregano
- Salt and pepper, to taste

Directions:

1. To achieve the perfect al dente texture, carefully follow the package instructions for boiling the fusilli pasta. Once cooked, drain the pasta and cool it down by rinsing it with cold water.
2. Gather a large mixing bowl and add the cooked and cooled fusilli pasta, cherry tomatoes, cucumber, Kalamata olives, feta cheese, parsley, and mint. Combine all these ingredients together for a delicious and refreshing pasta salad.
3. Combine the balsamic vinegar, olive oil, Dijon mustard, minced garlic, dried oregano, salt, and pepper in a small bowl. Vigorously whisk the ingredients together to produce a delicious and flavorful balsamic vinaigrette.

4. Drizzle the balsamic vinaigrette over the pasta salad and mix thoroughly to ensure that all the ingredients are evenly coated.
5. Taste and adjust the seasoning with additional salt and pepper, if needed.
6. Place a cover on the bowl and place the pasta salad in the refrigerator for a minimum of 1 hour to enable the flavors to blend harmoniously.
7. Before serving, give the pasta salad a good stir and garnish with additional fresh basil and parsley, if desired.
8. Serve the Mediterranean Pasta Salad with Balsamic Vinaigrette chilled, and enjoy!

Nutritional breakdown per serving:

Calories: 350 kcal, Protein: 10 grams, Carbohydrates: 50 grams, Fat: 12 grams, Saturated Fat: 3 grams, Cholesterol: 45 milligrams, Sodium: 450 milligrams, Fiber: 4 grams, and Sugar: 4 grams.

MEDITERRANEAN PASTA SALAD WITH HERBED YOGURT DRESSING

- Total Cooking Time: 20 minutes
- Prep Time: 10 minutes
- Servings: 4

Ingredients:

- 8 ounces fusilli pasta
- 1 cup cherry tomatoes, halved
- 1/2 cup sliced cucumber
- Use 1/2 cup of pitted and halved Kalamata olives
- 1/4 cup crumbled feta cheese
- 2 tablespoons chopped fresh parsley
- 2 tablespoons chopped fresh mint
- 1/4 cup plain Greek yogurt
- 1 tablespoon lemon juice
- 1 tablespoon extra virgin olive oil
- 1 clove garlic, minced
- Salt and pepper to taste

Directions:

1. To achieve the perfect al dente texture, carefully follow the package instructions for boiling the fusilli pasta. Once cooked, drain the pasta and cool it down by rinsing it with cold water.
2. Gather a large mixing bowl and add the cooked and cooled fusilli pasta, cherry tomatoes, cucumber, Kalamata olives, feta cheese, parsley, and mint. Combine all these ingredients together for a delicious and refreshing pasta salad.
3. In a small bowl, bring together the Greek yogurt, lemon juice, extra virgin olive oil, minced garlic, salt, and pepper. Whisk the ingredients until they blend harmoniously, creating a delectable dressing. To attain the ideal harmony of flavors, make sure to thoroughly blend all the components together. This will ensure that each element is evenly distributed throughout, resulting in a perfect balance of tastes.
4. Pour the herbed yogurt dressing over the pasta salad and toss gently to coat all the ingredients.
5. Take a moment to sample the dish and make any necessary adjustments to the seasoning based on your preferences.

6. Serve the Mediterranean Pasta Salad with Herbed Yogurt Dressing immediately or refrigerate for a few hours to let the flavors meld together.

Nutritional breakdown per serving:

Calories: 280 kcal, Protein: 10 grams, Carbohydrates: 42 grams, Fat: 8 grams, Saturated Fat: 3 grams, Cholesterol: 10 milligrams, Sodium: 320 milligrams, Fiber: 4 grams, and Sugar: 3 grams.

CHAPTER 10: SWEET PASTA DESSERTS

HONEY CINNAMON PASTA DESSERT

- Total Cooking Time: 15 minutes
- Prep Time: 5 minutes
- Servings: 4

Ingredients:

- Use 8 oz of spaghetti or angel hair pasta
- 2 tablespoons of unsalted butter
- 1/4 cup of honey
- 1 teaspoon of ground cinnamon
- 1/4 cup of chopped nuts, optional
- Fresh mint leaves for garnish (optional)

Directions:

1. To cook the pasta, carefully follow the instructions provided on the package. After achieving the desired texture and doneness of the pasta, carefully remove the excess water by draining it, and set the pasta aside to be used at a later time.
2. Place a large skillet on the stove over medium heat and continue heating the butter until it is fully melted.
3. Incorporate the cooked pasta into the skillet and delicately toss it to ensure an even coating with the melted butter.
4. Drizzle the honey over the pasta and sprinkle with ground cinnamon. Toss again to distribute the flavors evenly.
5. If desired, add the chopped nuts and toss once more to incorporate them into the dish.
6. Keep cooking the pasta for an additional 2-3 minutes, stirring occasionally, until it is completely heated and the flavors have fully merged.
7. Take the skillet off the heat and allow the pasta to cool down for a brief period before it is prepared for serving.
8. Garnish with fresh mint leaves for a touch of freshness.
9. Serve the Honey Cinnamon Pasta Dessert warm and enjoy!

Nutritional breakdown per serving:

Calories: 300 kcal, Protein: 25 grams, Carbohydrates: 55 grams, Fat: 8 grams, Saturated Fat: 4 grams, Cholesterol: 15 milligrams, Sodium: 75 milligrams, Fiber: 2 grams, and Sugar: 25 grams.

LEMON RICOTTA PASTA DESSERT

- Total Cooking Time: 15 minutes
- Prep Time: 5 minutes
- Servings: 4

Ingredients:

- 8 ounces of linguine or spaghetti
- 1 cup of ricotta cheese
- Zest of 1 lemon
- Juice of 1 lemon
- 1/4 cup of honey
- 1/4 cup of sliced almonds
- Fresh mint leaves for garnish (optional)

Directions:

1. To prepare the pasta, simply follow the instructions provided on the package. Once the pasta is cooked, drain it and set it aside for later use.
2. Combine the ricotta cheese, lemon zest, lemon juice, and honey in a spacious bowl. Mix the ingredients vigorously until they are thoroughly blended and evenly combined.
3. With a gentle touch, place the cooked pasta into the bowl and delicately toss it, ensuring that every strand is coated evenly with the lemon ricotta mixture.
4. Place a small skillet on the stovetop over medium heat, then add the sliced almonds to the pan. Toast them for 2-3 minutes, stirring occasionally, until they become golden brown and fragrant.
5. Sprinkle the toasted almonds over the pasta and toss again to incorporate them into the dish.
6. Allow the pasta to cool for a few minutes before serving.
7. To enhance the taste and add a touch of freshness, you have the option to garnish with fresh mint leaves, if you prefer.
8. Serve the Lemon Ricotta Pasta Dessert warm and enjoy!

Nutritional breakdown per serving:

Calories: 400 kcal, Protein: 15 grams, Carbohydrates: 55 grams, Fat: 15 grams, Saturated Fat: 6 grams, Cholesterol: 30 milligrams, Sodium: 100 milligrams, Fiber: 3 grams, and Sugar: 20 grams.

CHOCOLATE HAZELNUT PASTA DESSERT

- Total Cooking Time: 20 minutes
- Prep Time: 10 minutes
- Servings: 4

Ingredients:

- 8 ounces of fettuccine or spaghetti
- 1/2 cup of chocolate hazelnut spread
- 1/4 cup of milk (any type)
- 1 tablespoon of unsalted butter
- 1/4 cup of roasted hazelnuts, chopped
- Whipped cream for garnish (optional)
- Chocolate shavings for garnish (optional)

Directions:

1. Follow the instructions on the pasta packaging to prepare it. After it has been cooked, drain the pasta and set it aside.
2. In a small saucepan, blend the chocolate hazelnut spread, milk, and butter together. Apply gentle heat to the mixture over low heat, stirring it consistently until it achieves a smooth and fully incorporated texture.
3. Transfer the cooked pasta into the saucepan and delicately combine it with the chocolate hazelnut sauce, making sure to evenly coat the pasta.
4. Keep cooking the pasta for an additional 2-3 minutes, stirring intermittently, until it is completely heated and the flavors have harmonized.
5. Take the saucepan off the heat and allow the pasta to cool for a brief period before serving.
6. Sprinkle the chopped roasted hazelnuts over the pasta and toss once more to incorporate them into the dish.
7. For those who prefer, you can enhance the dish by adding a dollop of whipped cream and a sprinkle of chocolate shavings, providing an additional element of indulgence.
8. Serve the Chocolate Hazelnut Pasta Dessert warm and enjoy!

Nutritional breakdown per serving:

Calories: 500 kcal, Protein: 9 grams, Carbohydrates: 6 grams, Fat: 25 grams, Saturated Fat: 8 grams, Cholesterol: 10 milligrams, Sodium: 100 milligrams, Fiber: 4 grams, and Sugar: 30 grams.

ORANGE ALMOND PASTA DESSERT

- Total Cooking Time: 30 minutes
- Prep Time: 10 minutes
- Servings: 4

Ingredients:

- 8 ounces linguine pasta
- 1 cup orange juice
- Zest of 1 orange
- 1/2 cup granulated sugar
- 1/2 cup almond meal
- 1/4 cup unsalted butter
- 1/4 teaspoon almond extract
- 1/4 cup sliced almonds, toasted
- Fresh mint leaves, for garnish

Directions:

1. Prepare the linguine pasta following the instructions on the package, cooking it until it is firm to the bite (al dente). After the pasta has been cooked thoroughly, gently remove any excess water by draining it, and then set it aside to be used later.
2. In a saucepan, mix together the orange juice, orange zest, and granulated sugar. Heat the mixture gently over medium heat, stirring continuously until it reaches a simmer and the sugar is fully dissolved. Let it simmer for around 5 minutes, allowing it to reduce slightly.
3. In a separate small skillet, melt the butter over medium heat. Add the almond meal and cook, stirring constantly, until golden brown and fragrant, about 3-4 minutes. Take the mixture off the heat and incorporate the almond extract by stirring it in.
4. Add the cooked linguine pasta to the orange juice mixture and toss until well coated. Continue cooking for an extra 2-3 minutes, giving the pasta time to soak up the flavors.
5. Remove the pasta from heat and divide it into serving bowls. Drizzle each serving with the almond butter mixture and sprinkle with toasted sliced almonds.
6. Garnish with fresh mint leaves for a pop of color and added freshness.
7. Serve warm and enjoy!

Nutritional breakdown per serving:

Calories: 370 kcal, Protein: 7 grams, Carbohydrates: 55 grams, Fat: 15 grams, Saturated Fat: 6 grams, Cholesterol: 20 milligrams, Sodium: 10 milligrams, Fiber: 3 grams, and Sugar: 25 grams.

STRAWBERRY BALSAMIC PASTA DESSERT

- Total Cooking Time: 25 minutes
- Prep Time: 10 minutes
- Servings: 4

Ingredients:

- 8 ounces fettuccine pasta
- 1 cup fresh strawberries, sliced
- 2 tablespoons balsamic vinegar
- 2 tablespoons honey
- 1/4 cup mascarpone cheese
- 1/4 cup sliced almonds, toasted
- Fresh mint leaves, for garnish

Directions:

1. Prepare the fettuccine pasta by closely adhering to the instructions given on the package, ensuring it is cooked to the desired al dente texture. Once the pasta is ready, drain it and set it aside for future use.
2. To prepare the strawberry mixture, mix together the sliced strawberries, balsamic vinegar, and honey in a small bowl. Toss gently to coat the strawberries. Let them marinate for 5 minutes to allow the flavors to meld.
3. To toast the sliced almonds, use a separate small skillet and heat it over medium heat until the almonds turn golden brown and release a fragrant aroma. Once toasted, remove the almonds from the skillet and set them aside for later use.
4. To bring together the cooked fettuccine pasta and the marinated strawberries, place them in a spacious mixing bowl and gently combine them until well incorporated. Toss gently to incorporate the flavors.
5. Add the mascarpone cheese to the pasta mixture and gently stir until it is evenly distributed and coats the pasta strands.
6. Divide the pasta dessert into serving bowls. Sprinkle the toasted sliced almonds on top for added crunch and flavor.
7. Garnish with fresh mint leaves for a refreshing touch.

Nutritional breakdown per serving:

Calories: 390 kcal, Protein: 8 grams, Carbohydrates: 63 grams, Fat: 12 grams, Saturated Fat: 5 grams, Cholesterol: 20 milligrams, Sodium: 55 milligrams, Fiber: 4 grams, and Sugar: 15 grams.

PISTACHIO ROSEWATER PASTA DESSERT

- Preparation Time: 15 minutes
- Cooking Time: 15 minutes
- Servings: 4

Ingredients:

- 8 ounces fettuccine pasta
- 1 cup shelled pistachios, chopped
- 1/2 cup heavy cream
- 1/4 cup granulated sugar
- 2 tablespoons rosewater
- 1 tablespoon unsalted butter
- 1/4 teaspoon ground cardamom
- Pinch of salt
- Crushed pistachios, for garnish
- Dried rose petals, for garnish

Directions:

1. To cook the fettuccine pasta, carefully adhere to the instructions provided on the package until it reaches the desired al dente texture. After cooking, strain the pasta and place it aside for future use.
2. To melt the butter, use a large skillet and heat it over medium heat. Add the chopped pistachios to the skillet and cook for 2-3 minutes, stirring regularly, until they turn slightly golden and emit a pleasant aroma.
3. Reduce heat to simmer. Add cream, sugar, rosewater, cardamom, and salt to skillet. Stir well. Simmer for 5 minutes to blend flavors.
4. Gently combine the cooked fettuccine pasta with the pistachio rosewater sauce in the skillet, ensuring that the pasta is evenly coated. Continue cooking for an extra 2-3 minutes, occasionally stirring, until the pasta is thoroughly heated.
5. Take the skillet off the heat and portion out the Pistachio Rosewater Pasta Dessert onto individual serving plates. For an elegant touch, adorn with crushed pistachios and dried rose petals.

Nutritional breakdown per serving:

Calories: 480 kcal, Protein: 10 grams, Carbohydrates: 56 grams, Fat: 24 grams, Saturated Fat: 10 grams, Cholesterol: 50 milligrams, Sodium: 35 milligrams, Fiber: 4 grams, and Sugar: 16 grams.

COCONUT MANGO PASTA DESSERT

- Preparation Time: 15 minutes
- Cooking Time: 15 minutes
- Servings: 4

Ingredients:

- 8 ounces linguine pasta
- 1 ripe mango, peeled and diced
- 1 cup coconut milk
- 1/4 cup granulated sugar
- 2 tablespoons lime juice
- 1 tablespoon coconut oil
- 1/4 teaspoon vanilla extract
- Pinch of salt
- Toasted coconut flakes, for garnish
- Fresh mint leaves, for garnish

Directions:

1. For a perfectly al dente texture, it is important to diligently adhere to the instructions provided on the package when cooking the linguine pasta. Once cooked to perfection, drain the pasta and set it aside for future use.
2. In a blender, combine the diced mango, coconut milk, granulated sugar, lime juice, coconut oil, vanilla extract, and a pinch of salt. Blend until smooth and creamy.
3. In a large skillet, heat the mango-coconut sauce over medium heat. Bring it to a simmer and let it cook for about 5 minutes, stirring occasionally, until slightly thickened.
4. Combine cooked linguine pasta with the sauce in the skillet and gently toss to ensure even coating. Continue cooking the pasta for an extra 2-3 minutes, giving it an occasional stir, until it is completely heated through.
5. Take the skillet off the heat and distribute the Coconut Mango Pasta Dessert evenly among the serving plates. Enhance the tropical flavor by adorning it with toasted coconut flakes and fresh mint leaves as a garnish.

Nutritional breakdown per serving:

Calories: 380 kcal, Protein: 5 grams, Carbohydrates: 65 grams, Fat: 12 grams, Saturated Fat: 10 grams, Cholesterol: 0 milligrams, Sodium: 10 milligrams, Fiber: 4 grams, and Sugar: 28 grams.

CARAMELIZED APPLE PASTA DESSERT

- Prep Time: 15 minutes
- Cooking Time: 30 minutes
- Servings: 4

Ingredients:

- 8 oz spaghetti
- 2 tablespoons unsalted butter
- 4 peeled, cored, and thinly sliced medium apples
- 1/4 cup granulated sugar
- 1/2 teaspoon ground cinnamon
- 1/4 teaspoon ground nutmeg
- 1/2 cup heavy cream
- 1/4 cup caramel sauce
- 1/4 cup chopped walnuts (optional)
- Fresh mint leaves for garnish (optional)

Directions:

1. Before preparing the baking dish, make sure to adjust the oven temperature to 350°F (175°C). Next, lightly coat the dish with either butter or cooking spray to prevent sticking.
2. In a generously sized skillet, gently melt the butter over medium heat. Introduce the thinly sliced apples into the skillet and cook them for about 5 minutes, occasionally stirring, until they reach a tender consistency.
3. In a mixing bowl, gather the ricotta cheese, powdered sugar, vanilla extract, cinnamon, and nutmeg. Mix them together until thoroughly combined and the mixture achieves a smooth consistency.
4. Lower the heat to a gentle simmer and slowly pour in the heavy cream. Stir gently to combine with the caramelized apples. Cook for another 2-3 minutes, until the sauce thickens slightly.
5. Gently incorporate the cooked spaghetti into the skillet, ensuring that the pasta is evenly coated with the caramelized apple sauce.
6. Remove from heat and drizzle the caramel sauce over the pasta dessert. Toss again to incorporate the sauce evenly.
7. Divide the caramelized apple pasta dessert among serving plates. Sprinkle with chopped walnuts for added crunch, if desired.
8. Garnish with fresh mint leaves for a pop of color and freshness.

Nutritional breakdown per serving:

Calories: 420 kcal, Protein: 5 grams, Carbohydrates: 61 grams, Fat: 19 grams, Saturated Fat: 11 grams, Cholesterol: 60 milligrams, Sodium: 50 milligrams, Fiber: 5 grams, and Sugar: 32 grams.

RICOTTA STUFFED CANNELLONI DESSERT

- Prep Time: 20 minutes
- Cooking Time: 40 minutes
- Servings: 6

Ingredients:

- 12 cannelloni tubes
- 2 cups ricotta cheese
- 1 cup powdered sugar
- 1 teaspoon vanilla extract
- 1/2 teaspoon ground cinnamon
- 1/4 teaspoon ground nutmeg
- 1 cup heavy cream
- 1/4 cup unsalted butter, melted
- 1/4 cup chopped pistachios (optional)
- Powdered sugar for dusting

Directions:

1. Begin the process by preheating your oven to 350°F (175°C). After that, get a baking dish and either apply a thin layer of butter or coat it evenly using cooking spray.
2. Cook the cannelloni tubes according to package instructions until al dente. Drain and set aside.
3. In a mixing bowl, combine the ricotta cheese, powdered sugar, vanilla extract, cinnamon, and nutmeg. Stir until well combined and smooth.
4. Utilize either a piping bag or a spoon to stuff each cannelloni tube with the ricotta mixture. Place the filled cannelloni tubes in the greased baking dish.
5. In a small saucepan, heat the heavy cream and melted butter over low heat until warm. Pour the cream mixture over the stuffed cannelloni tubes, ensuring they are fully covered.
6. Position the stuffed cannelloni in the preheated oven and let them bake for around 30 to 35 minutes, or until they are fully cooked and the top surface turns a beautiful golden brown shade.
7. Take the dish out of the oven and allow it to cool for a brief period of time. Sprinkle with chopped pistachios for added texture and flavor, if desired.
8. Dust the top of the cannelloni dessert with powdered sugar before serving.

Nutritional breakdown per serving:

Calories: 540 kcal, Protein: 14 grams, Carbohydrates: 50 grams, Fat: 31 grams, Saturated Fat: 19 grams, Cholesterol: 110 milligrams, Sodium: 135 milligrams, Fiber: 1 grams, and Sugar: 26 grams.

NUTTY RAISIN PASTA DESSERT

- Total Cooking Time: 25 minutes
- Prep Time: 10 minutes
- Servings: 4

Ingredients:

- 8 ounces penne pasta
- 1 cup raisins
- 1/2 cup chopped walnuts
- 1/4 cup unsalted butter
- 1/4 cup honey
- 1/2 teaspoon cinnamon
- 1/4 teaspoon nutmeg
- 1/4 teaspoon salt
- Optional toppings: whipped cream, vanilla ice cream

Directions:

1. To cook the penne pasta, carefully adhere to the instructions on the package until it reaches the desired consistency of being firm to the bite (al dente). After cooking, carefully strain the pasta to remove excess water, and then set it aside for future use.
2. In a spacious frying pan, heat the butter over medium heat. Introduce the raisins and walnuts, and sauté for 2-3 minutes until the raisins become plump and the walnuts release an aromatic scent.
3. Lower the heat to a gentle setting and carefully mix in the honey, cinnamon, nutmeg, and salt. Cook for an additional 2-3 minutes until the mixture is well combined and heated through.
4. Incorporate the cooked penne pasta into the skillet and delicately toss it to ensure that the pasta is evenly coated with the raisin and walnut mixture. Continue cooking for an extra 2-3 minutes to allow the flavors to blend harmoniously.
5. Remove from heat and divide the pasta dessert into serving bowls.
6. Enjoy the dish while it's still warm, either as it is or enhance its presentation by adding a dollop of whipped cream or a generous scoop of creamy vanilla ice cream for a truly indulgent and satisfying final touch.

Nutritional breakdown per serving:

Calories: 420 kcal, Protein: 7 grams, Carbohydrates: 64 grams, Fat: 17 grams, Saturated Fat: 6 grams, Cholesterol: 20 milligrams, Sodium: 150 milligrams, Fiber: 4 grams, and Sugar: 31 grams.

CONCLUSION

In concluding this Mediterranean pizza and pasta cookbook, it's clear that the culinary traditions of the Mediterranean region offer a rich tapestry of flavors, ingredients, and techniques that have stood the test of time. From the simplicity of a classic Margherita pizza to the complexity of a seafood linguine, the recipes in this cookbook have showcased the diversity and vibrancy of Mediterranean cuisine.

As you've embarked on a journey through this cookbook, you've not only learned to create delicious dishes but also gained an appreciation for the cultural significance of each recipe. The use of fresh, seasonal ingredients, the emphasis on vibrant flavors, and the celebration of communal dining are all integral parts of the Mediterranean culinary experience.

Whether you're a seasoned cook or a beginner in the kitchen, we hope that the recipes in this cookbook have inspired you to explore the joys of Mediterranean cooking and to share memorable meals with your loved ones. May the aromas of basil, oregano, and olive oil continue to fill your kitchen, and may the spirit of the Mediterranean cuisine enrich your culinary adventures for years to come.

Thank you for taking this flavorful journey with us, and may your kitchen always be filled with the warmth and satisfaction that comes from preparing and enjoying Mediterranean pizza and pasta. Buon Appetito!

Made in the USA
Las Vegas, NV
16 December 2024

14172719R00122